TOILET TRAINING TO INDEPENDENCE FOR THE HANDICAPPED

A Manual for Trainers

SUE BETTISON

Mental Health Services
South Australia Health Commission
Adelaide, Australia

The result of extensive research and testing, this book details a program for toilet training mentally handicapped individuals. The manual begins with an overview of the development of bladder and bowel control. Initial assessment of toileting skills, behavior management, establishment of the training environment, selection of trainers, and professional and organizational support all receive thorough coverage. The program itself is presented in steps. Each step is detailed with respect to behavioral target, performance criteria and specific procedures. The author explains techniques for ensuring smooth performance of the entire toileting sequence, and she describes methods for maintaining the skills learned. A final section encompasses commonly encountered problems and their solutions. Appendices provide samples of record sheets and charts and instructions for their use. A bibliography also is included.

CHARLES C THOMAS • PUBLISHER • SPRINGFIELD • ILLINOIS • USA

TOILET TRAINING
TO INDEPENDENCE
FOR THE HANDICAPPED

"TOILET TRAINING TO INDEPENDENCE FOR THE HANDICAPPED"

A Manual for Trainers

By

SUE BETTISON

Mental Health Services
South Australia Health Commission
Adelaide, Australia

CHARLES C THOMAS • **PUBLISHER**
Springfield • *Illinois* • *U.S.A.*

Published and Distributed Throughout the World by

CHARLES C THOMAS · PUBLISHER

2600 South First Street

Springfield, Illinois 62717, U.S.A.

© *1982 by* CHARLES C THOMAS · PUBLISHER

ISBN 0-398-04678-6

Library of Congress Catalog Card Number: 82-807

*With THOMAS BOOKS careful attention is given to all details of
manufacturing and design. It is the Publisher's desire to present books that are
satisfactory as to their physical qualities and artistic possibilities and
appropriate for their particular use. THOMAS BOOKS will be true to those
laws of quality that assure a good name and good will.*

Printed in the United States of America

I-RX-1

Library of Congress Cataloging in Publication Data

Bettison, Sue.
   Toilet training to independence.

   Bibliography: p.
   1. Toilet training.   2. Handicapped children--Care
and treatment. I. Title.
HQ770.5.B47   649'.62   82-807
ISBN 0-398-04678-6   AACR2

ACKNOWLEDGMENTS

THIS MANUAL IS THE RESULT OF THE HARD work and dedication of many people. I especially thank the children who worked hard to learn new skills while we were testing this programme. They have made it possible for other handicapped persons to benefit from their success. They also taught us a great deal and freely shared with us their affection, trust, and sense of fun.

No one could have worked harder and with more dedication than the parents, Intensive Training Unit staff, and volunteers who helped train the children. Their consideration, attention to detail, and belief in the value of the programme played a large part in its success. Special recognition is due to Jackie Ryjoch and Brenda Hankins, who kept the programme running smoothly. I also wish to thank Ian Kaines of the Family Training Unit, who provided and serviced the alarms, Denise Skinner, Janice Clarke, Roxanne Hookes, Liz Antonergios, and Chris Lelifani, who helped assess the children before and after training, Ted Nettlebeck, Eric Rump, and Bob Wilson, who advised on research design and data analysis, and Maria Raptis, Liz Antonergios, and Chris Lelifani, who acted as interpreters for one Greek-speaking family. Tracy Byrne, Nancy McCarthy, and Angela Steinberner helped with typing, layout, and artwork, and Charles Hart designed the alarms. Many others also took an interest and gave valuable advice during the project.

The intensive toilet-training project was whole heartedly supported by Strathmont Centre, which provided staff and resources in line with an enlightened policy of training and rehabilitation. Approval and support were also provided by the South Australian Health Commission and the University of Adelaide.

CONTENTS

TOILET TRAINING
TO INDEPENDENCE
FOR THE HANDICAPPED

Chapter 1

INTRODUCTION

IN THE LAST TWO DECADES, THE ATTITUDE TO incontinence among handicapped persons has changed dramatically. Incontinence is no longer regarded as an inevitable part of severe handicap that must be tolerated and kept out of public view. It is now recognized that most incontinence is a result of learning difficulties, which can often be overcome with specially designed, systematic teaching. It is also recognized that some incontinence is a direct result of overprotection, inconsistent handling, institutionalization, and low expectations.

This change in attitude has both led to and been fostered by the development of systematic and effective toilet-training methods. Since 1960 there have appeared over ninety published papers and books describing research or service programmes whose aim was to provide effective training in daytime bladder and bowel control. The early reports were of relatively simple procedures, but there has been a significant trend towards more complex and systematic methods. Most programmes are based on behavioural principles, although they differ markedly in the actual training procedures used.

Since 1973 a small team of staff within the Intellectually Retarded Services has been developing a wide range of training programmes for the intellectually handicapped in South Australia. The development of toilet-training programmes has been a major project. The initial stages involved trials of a number of programmes reported in the literature, together with the establishment of two specialized training units and the training of people to staff them. Some of the trials were primarily service oriented; others were fully controlled research programmes.

During this time we worked with a wide variety of clients. They ranged from four to fifty years of age. They included nonhandicapped children and persons with all levels of intellectual handicap as well as a variety of physical, sensory, and learning disabilities. Training took place in their own homes, in schools, and in institutions and was carried out by parents, teachers, institution staff, psychologists, physiotherapists, paramedical aides, and volunteers. Our experience with these clients has shown us that there are many different reasons for incontinence. Differences exist in the number and kind of toileting skills which are lacking, in the learning difficulties and physical disabilities which interfere with learning and performance, and in the environmental influences on learning. These differences cannot be catered for by one, packaged toilet-training programme. Effective toilet-training services need to offer a variety of programmes that can be matched to the needs of each client.

The two units between them now provide a range of programmes and training environments to suit a wide variety of needs. The *Intensive Training Unit* is based in the residential training institution, Strathmont Centre, and provides a highly controlled learning environment, individual training for clients, and specializes in consultation and staff training. The work of this unit has resulted in a significant decrease in the number of incontinent residents in the institution and is now able to offer places to nonresidents and their families. The *Family Training Unit* specializes in teaching parents and others working with handicapped persons to run their own programmes within normal daily routines. In addition, members of the two units provide consultation and advice to schools, community health centres, and other centres for handicapped persons.

A few clients had special problems or lived in situations that could not be overcome even with the range of programme choices that were available. These clients helped extend our understanding of the nature of the toileting process. As a result, several new programmes and techniques were developed. The Intensive Training Unit developed a complex bladder-training programme especially for profoundly and severely intellectually handicapped children with severe learning difficulties. The Family Training Unit developed a programme that parents could use to teach young children to indicate when they needed to go to the toilet (Kaines, 1979). Bowel-training programmes were developed for children who were bladder trained but still soiled or suffered from constipation. A variety of potty and pants alarms and reward devices were developed that could be assembled cheaply and which were light, durable, and reliable. Some of these are now made by intellectually handicapped adults in sheltered workshops. Two of these devices are described in Appendix A.

The programme described in this manual was also developed in this way. Initially, we planned to provide the Azrin and Foxx programme for profoundly and severely intellectually handicapped clients who needed both extensive practice and training in all the component skills of toileting (Azrin and Foxx, 1971; Foxx and Azrin, 1973). During 1975 and 1976, we offered this programme to forty residents at Strathmont Centre.

The first trials were published (Bettison, Davison, Taylor, and Fox, 1976), and further papers are in preparation. We found that the programme was effective for many clients, but for others progress through the stages of the programme was too rapid. Some were confused by the teaching of many skills at the same time. The programme did not teach all the componenets of sphincter control. In addition, the component skills were not adequately joined in a smooth sequence.

This programme attempts to overcome these problems. It has been designed to meet the needs of handicapped persons who have progressed at least some way beyond uncontrolled reflex voiding, but are not progressing further with the training techniques commonly used by parents, teachers, and institution staff. Occasionally, it has been useful for children who are continuing to learn new toileting skills, but whose slow progress is denying them access to appropriate educational and developmental opportunities. It has been specially designed to overcome many of the learning difficulties resulting from handicap. It was tested by the Intensive Training Unit during 1979 and 1980 with twenty intellectually handicapped children. Half of them lived at home and half were resident in Strathmont Centre. During the trials, we limited training time to thirty-four days for experimental purposes. Of the twenty children, ten completed training successfully, three had not completed the last phase but achieved complete mastery during the Maintenance Phase in their normal environments, and six more had not completed the last one or two phases but probably would have if they had been given more time. They are now mostly accident free and often toilet themselves. The remaining child did not progress past the first phase and was discovered during training to have severe visual deficits, which were not accommodated by the programme.

We do not expect 100 percent success with all clients, even when no time limit is placed on training. As with any teaching programme, there is still room for improvement. Some of the problems still requiring solutions are outlined in Chapter 6, "Common Problems and How to Handle Them." You may find others as you use the programme. We are sure that there is more to learn about the nature of bladder and bowel control. We are also sure that further refinements in training techniques are possible. We hope that some of you will carry on our work by further analysing the component skills that are involved in self-toileting and testing improved procedures for teaching them. However, with the present state of knowledge and techniques, few handicapped persons need remain incontinent. The problem now is not primarily lack of effective techniques, but rather service and funding priorities.

Chapter 2
HANDICAP AND THE
DEVELOPMENT OF SELF-TOILETING

SELF-CONTROL OF toileting is a learned skill that is usually acquired with little formal teaching. It involves a sequence of skills that appear to be learned in much the same order by most children, although how quickly each skill is acquired varies a great deal. Acquisition of these skills depends on the gradual neurological and physiological maturation that occurs during the first few years of life.

THE DEVELOPMENT OF BLADDER AND BOWEL CONTROL

1. Infants begin life with reflex emptying of the bladder and bowel. This reflex is triggered by the filling of the bladder or bowel, which sets off rhythmical contractions leading to voiding, over which the infant has no control. Bladder and bowel capacity is small, so that small amounts are voided frequently. For instance, about twenty-nine cubic centimetres of urine are voided roughly seventeen times a day during the first few months of life. However, frequency of voiding can vary considerably, depending on fluid and food intake, activity, temperature, and general health.

2. With further maturing of the nervous system during the first year or two of life, young children begin to show awareness of the sensations of a full bladder or bowel. The first signs of awareness are often seen in such behaviour as a look of concentration while all activity stops, crossing legs, fidgeting, grizzling, holding one or both hands between legs, or saying the common word for voiding or toilet. Intellectual handicap or damage to the nervous system may interfere with the development of awareness of bladder and bowel tension, thus making it difficult for the person to learn bladder and bowel control. It is this awareness that enables the child to first begin holding back voiding for a brief time when the bladder or bowel is full, so that the first steps in toilet training, i.e. to get to the toilet or pot, can be taught. Conscious holding back of voiding is helped by a gradually increasing bladder and bowel capacity. By the second year, the amount of urine voided has usually doubled and the number of voidings per day has reduced. However, the act of voiding itself is still automatic and dependent on a full bladder or bowel.

6

3. By three years of age, most children have learned to resist emptying their bowels until it suits them. Even if they are not using the toilet or pot at this stage, they usually choose to be private, which is just as clearly evidence of bowel control. At this age most children have also learned to hold back urine for a considerable time when the bladder is full. This requires conscious control of perineal muscles. These form a saddle of muscle running from front to back between the legs. They are tightened, raising the bladder neck and thus closing the ring of muscle (sphincter) at the opening of the bladder. The perineal muscles are used in the same way to close the bowel sphincter. This action effectively prevents urine or faeces from passing through. This holding ability, together with a further increase in bladder capacity, means that children pass a greater quantity of urine at any one time and only void about eight or nine times a day. However, although the ability to hold the sphincter closed to prevent voiding has been acquired, children at this stage cannot fully control relaxing of the spinchter so that voiding can begin. They often have to wait until attention is taken by other things, when the perineal muscles will automatically relax and reflex voiding will occur. This incomplete voluntary control is clearly seen when young children are taken to the toilet, do not void, go back to play, and immediately wet or soil.

4. During the fourth year, most children learn to voluntarily start voiding from a full bowel or bladder. To do this requires taking a small breath and holding it, tightening the abdominal muscles, relaxing the perineal muscles, then pushing down slightly with the thoracic diaphragm. Once children acquire this skill they will be able to void within a few seconds, given that the bladder or bowel is full. By this stage, too, children can interrupt the urine stream at will and often take great delight in experimenting with the flow. As a result of the two new skills and a further increase in bladder capacity, the occasional wet pants that most toilet-trained children experience during the earlier stages of learning no longer occur, and many children can remain dry through the night.

5. The final control is not fully accomplished until about six years of age when starting the urine flow from a partly full bladder is acquired. This requires a finer coordination of diaphragm, abdominal, and perineal muscles. This new skill allows children to go to the toilet at almost any time and void, no matter how small an amount has accumulated in the bladder. Even though bladder capacity has almost reached the adult level, the amount of urine passed will vary greatly, depending on how full the bladder is. Children with this skill can be reasonably expected to go to the toilet and use it before an outing.

THE EFFECTS OF HANDICAP

Although this outline is brief, it indicates that learning bladder and bowel control is far from simple. It is not surprising that wetting, soiling, and other toileting problems are fairly common among both children and adults. Nevertheless, most children progress through the developmental stages and learn to toilet themselves with very little assistance. Many handicapped children also learn these skills with no difficulty. However, failure to learn toileting skills is a major problem for a considerable number of both children and adults with handicaps. Intellectually handicapped children by definition develop more slowly than nonhandicapped children and, consequently, acquire bladder and bowel control later. Generally, the acquisition of toileting skills occurs more slowly the greater the intellectual handicap, so that many severely and profoundly retarded persons remain totally or partially incontinent well into adulthood. Furthermore, many forms of handicap involve specific deficits in sensory functions, the focusing and sustaining of attention, motor control, perception, and understanding, all of which may interfere with the learning of toileting skills. Additional neurological and physical abnormalities affecting the urinary tract and bowel are also relatively common among handicapped persons, and these make control of voiding especially difficult.

Our culture adds further learning tasks to those of bladder and bowel control. We require that children learn which places are acceptable for toileting and how to find them, even in strange surroundings. They must learn to remove and replace pants, flush toilets, use toilet tissue, and wash their hands. Complete control requires that they also anticipate periods when free access to the toilet is unlikely and plan their toileting accordingly. There are a number of complex discriminations and motor sequences involved in these tasks that add further to the learning difficulties experienced by many handicapped persons.

Full independence in toileting only occurs when the control of bladder and bowel is joined to the socially required toileting skills, and both are controlled by fine discriminations of internal sensations and external cues. The actual sequencing of this complex set of skills creates further difficulties for many handicapped persons, such that they only perform some parts of the sequence, or perform the parts in the wrong order.

Because of the learning difficulties that handicaps impose, many handicapped persons do not learn to control their own toileting without special teaching methods designed specifically to overcome their particular learning problem. Many handicapped persons require direct training of some or all of the components of internal bladder and bowel control, as well as the socially required toileting skills. They may need direct training to increase bladder capacity, awareness of bladder or bowel tension, the ability to hold back voiding, and to voluntarily start voiding after holding it back. They may also need detailed training in handling clothing, sitting correctly on the toilet, concentrating on voiding, and recognizing when voiding is finished. In addition, many handicapped persons can only learn these toileting skills if other more general skills are taught. They may need to be taught to pay attention, increase their concentration span, finish tasks that have begun, and make independent decisions rather than asking for direction. Many may need considerable practice before a newly learned skill becomes habitual. Many learn to control their own toileting but require special teaching before they can use these skills during their normal daily activities.

Additional handicaps often interfere with self-toileting that are not directly related to any impairments that the handicapped person may have. Some handicapped persons are actively prevented from learning toileting skills, or from using skills that they already possess, by the negative expectations and ineffective teaching methods of those who care for them or by restrictions in their environment. While these are generally due to lack of realistic information and advice, they nevertheless impose unnecessary failure and dependence on the handicapped person and considerable hardship and frustration on caregivers. We have had a number of children referred to us for toilet training who were discovered to have all the toileting skills and yet did not toilet themselves and continued to have voiding accidents. They lived in situations where the label of retardation led others to assume that they were incapable of learning normally. Accidents were accepted as inevitable, and parents, direct-care staff, or teachers continued to direct and help them with most toileting activities so that they had little opportunity to use their skills independently.

Other children were inadvertently but systematically taught to have voiding accidents. Observation of these children and their situation showed that toileting was often associated with discomfort and unhappiness. Frequent trips to the toilet interrupted pleasurable activities as often as twelve or more times a day in some cases. Children were often made to stay on the toilet for long periods of time. Toileting was frequently associated with scolding for accidents, for failure to void in the toilet, or for not remaining still. Children were somtimes required to balance precariously or sit for so long that their buttocks became sore. Furthermore, recognition and praise were rarely given when voiding did occur in the toilet. This was in contrast to the events associated with voiding accidents when ten minutes or so of physical contact, conversation, and attention were given while the children were cleaned up and changed. There were also some children who had voiding accidents in order to avoid unpleasant or stressful situations or to gain the attention of an adult. The problem for these children was generally not a lack of toileting skills, but rather that they had received reward for having accidents.

Some children, especially those in institutional or school settings, had accidents because they could not open the door that led to the toilet or because doors were kept locked during some parts of the day. Furthermore, toilets in some schools were so sited that children could not go to them without supervision. Toilet areas were often cold and very noisy when groups of children were taken to the toilet together. Staff changes in institutions frequently disrupted the children's routine and prevented staff members from designing and carrying out simple, consistent toilet training procedures that were suited to each child. Instead, children were subjected to procedures which enabled staff to manage children as a group and which changed with each new staff change. New members of staff who did not know the children had little opportunity to learn about their abilities and needs and therefore frequently responded inappropriately. Children who needed no help were often taken to the toilet when they did not need to go, and those who had some but not all of the toileting skills often had everything done for them.

It is clear that the wide variety of reasons for incontinence among handicapped persons requires a variety of solutions. Some of these will largely involve changes in the attitudes and human management skills of caregivers, some will require physical, administrative, or policy changes for services, and others will be by way of training for the handicapped person. Sometimes all of these solutions will be necessary. In addition, a variety of toilet-training programmes are necessary that have proven effectiveness in overcoming the range of skill deficits and learning problems that are found among handicapped persons. The level of development in bladder and bowel control is of particular importance in determining which programme is most suitable. For instance, independent, accident-free self-toileting is unlikely to be acquired by a person who is unaware of bladder or bowel tension and who cannot hold back voiding for a short period once the bladder or bowel is full. On the other hand, a person who has most of the toileting skills but still has occasional accidents will probably quickly become accident-free with little more than systematic reward for toilet use.

The most suitable training programme is best determined by detailed assessment of the toileting skills, deficits, and situation of each person. This manual is not primarily concerned with procedures to encourage attitude and administrative change, but rather with the learning difficulties of incontinent persons. The assessment of skills and deficits for the programme in this manual is described in the next chapter. Many of the assessment procedures described are also useful when the choice is between a variety of training procedures and programmes.

Chapter 3
ASSESSMENT

MANY PARENTS, TEACHERS, AND INSTITUTION staff persevere for years with handicapped children and adults who wet or soil. They spend considerable time in cleaning up after accidents and taking their charges to the toilet. They often feel convinced that, because the handicapped person has not become fully independent with the usual toileting routines, he is unable to learn any further toileting skills. Consequently, the methods they use in relation to toileting are aimed at reducing the mess that has to be cleaned up rather than at teaching new skills. However, once it is known that successful toilet-training programmes are available, referrals for this service accumulate rapidly.

This programme is not suitable for all handicapped persons referred for toilet training. Some will have extreme disabilities that are likely to prevent them from benefitting from toilet training. Others will have few or no toileting skills and require training to establish initial bladder and bowel control rather than independent self-toileting. Some need toilet training, but their living environment or current levels of toileting skill suggest that a less intensive programme will be successful.

Your assessment task will, therefore, include two stages. The first is to decide whether the handicapped person is likely to benefit from this programme. The second occurs once the person is accepted and involves a detailed assessment of both the level of skill in each toileting task, together with the selection of suitable rewards and the development of behaviour management procedures.

Who Is Suitable for Training?

The initial assessment should establish a number of things: that the handicapped person is clearly not controlling his own toileting; which of the bladder- and bowel-control skills are absent; whether there is any neurological or physical impairment in functions that are required for self-toileting; and what level of toileting skill would be allowed and supported by the person's environment and the other people in it. This information is initially provided by interviewing those people who have the major responsibility for the handicapped person. This may include the parent(s) if the person lives at home, the teacher if the person attends school, and institution staff if the person lives in a residential facility. The interview should cover the following.

11

Information for the Caregiver

Describe the programme and the assessment briefly, explaining what it entails. The caregiver also needs to know approximately how long training will take, how it will effect other aspects of the person's life, who will be involved as trainers, and the amount and kind of involvement expected of the caregiver and other people in the person's environment such as family members, teachers, and therapists. Each person involved with the handicapped person will need to understand that training, to be effective, should be continuous, and that major medication changes, hospitalization, or major changes in caregivers during maintenance may seriously interfere with successful learning.

You and the caregiver can then decide whether the programme is feasible. It is often necessary to give this information to a number of people involved with the handicapped person. Occasionally, one wants to use the programme, but others do not. Disagreements such as these need to be resolved before training is offered.

Usually, handicapped persons who are incontinent are young children or are severely intellectually handicapped and without sufficient capacity to understand the nature of the programme. However, if a handicapped person is referred for toilet training and also has sufficient capacity to understand, she or he should receive the same information as the caregiver(s) and should be the person who decides on the feasibility of the programme.

The Balthazar Adaptive-Behaviour Scale for Toileting

This is a standardized assessment of toileting skill. Because it is standardized, it allows a comparison of one individual with another. Although it does not assess all the component skills involved in toileting, it is the best and simplest predictor of success during toilet training that we have found.

The Balthazar Adaptive-Behaviour Scales assess a number of skills and behaviours (Balthazar, 1971). It is the toileting questionnaire that is used in this assessment. The complete set of scales and manuals can be obtained in Australia by writing to the Distribution Services Division, Australian Council of Educational Research, P.O. Box 210, Hawthorn, Victoria, 3122, or by ordering directly from Research Press Company, 2612 North Mattis Avenue, Champaign, Illinois, 61820, U.S.A.

The toileting questionnarie contains twelve questions about daytime and nighttime toileting. It is filled in during the interview with the major caregiver(s). Although the questions are straightforward, it is often necessary to ask further probe questions to ensure that the caregiver's replies and your scoring are as accurate as possible. Occasionally, a caregiver finds it impossible to answer one or more of the questions. In this case, it may be necessary to arrange for a record of those behaviours to be kept by the caregiver throughout the week. The scale is only as accurate as your skill and care in eliciting the information will allow. Therefore, it is wise to read the manual carefully and practice using the questionnaire several times before including it as part of the assessment for toilet training.

The eight questions relating to daytime toileting alone together indicate whether a handicapped person can benefit from this programme. The possible scores on the daytime toileting section range from 0 - 70. We have found that a score of 14 or less describes persons who generally require basic bladder and bowel training and are not yet ready to learn independent toileting skills. We have also found that a score of 40 or more describes persons who generally have enough skills to become fully independent with less intensive training than is provided by this programme. Some handicapped persons who score between 15 and 39 often toilet themselves successfully, but still have accidents. This indicates that the person has many of the skills, but that these have not yet been attached reliably as a sequence to the awareness of bladder or bowel tension. However, we have occasionally accepted handicapped persons with a score between 15 and 39 who have not achieved full success during training, although they have usually improved considerably. We suggest that the scores from this scale be considered carefully, together with the other information gathered during assessment.

If a handicapped person scores below 15, he or she is usually unable to benefit from this programme. A person who scores above 39 has enough toileting skills to benefit from much less intensive training. However, you may need to carry the interview further in order to advise on other action or programmes that may be useful. If the score falls between 15 and 39, continue with the following assessment interview.

Questions to Ask

The initial interview with staff or parents provides further valuable information. Answers to the following questions can indicate the presence of physical problems and alert you to special training needs.

The answers to questions one to six indicate the level of development in bladder and bowel control. Normally, we do not recommend toilet training for a handicapped child under four years of age. However, some older handicapped persons may still be functioning like an infant under two years of age in terms of bladder and bowel control. The decision then is whether to wait for them to mature further or to directly attempt to increase bladder capacity and awareness of bladder and bowel tension. This programme is not appropriate in these cases. Before deciding on such training you will need specialist medical assistance to determine whether there are physiological problems that may prevent the person from learning these skills. If the pattern of voiding is unusual for a person of about that age, it is wise to have the urine or faeces tested. Routine urinalysis, including specific gravity, and microfaeces culture will usually show up any infection, parasites, or common diseases. These should be treated before toilet training is considered. In addition, extreme frequency of urination can be, in rare cases, the result of an abnormally wide bladder neck, sphincter malfunction, or kidney or ureter malfunction. If these are suspected, the person should be examined by a urologist. Abnormal bowel functioning can be the result of long-term constipation, inadequate diet, or one of a number of physical or metabolic problems.

1. How frequently does voiding occur? More than eight or nine times a day on the average may indicate low bladder capacity. Several bowel movements a day may indicate an immature bowel or other problems. Bowel movements that occur only every few days may indicate constipation, especially if it is accompanied by slight but frequent smearing of the pants.

2. Does the person show that he or she is aware of bladder or bowel tension? Letting another person know that he or she wants to go to the toilet is the clearest sign of this awareness, but there may be other signs.

3. Are there any signs that the person recognizes when voiding has started and stopped?

4. Does the person ever void only small amounts of urine or faeces in the pants when accidents occur? This indicates that there is some ability to briefly hold back voiding when the bladder or bowel is full. In the absence of constipation, it also indicates awareness of the beginning of voiding.

5. How long does it take for voiding in the toilet to occur after sitting? Regular voiding within seconds of sitting on the toilet indicates the ability to voluntarily relax the sphincter.

6. How much is voided in the toilet or during accidents? Varying amounts of urine, together with immediate voiding in the toilet, indicates complete bladder control. Consistently small and frequent amounts can indicate low bladder capacity, a physical problem requiring treatment, or incomplete control of sphincter relaxation.

7. Does the person ever go to the pot or toilet without direction?

8. How much verbal or physical help is required to get the pants up and down?

9. How much verbal or physical help is required for sitting and remaining seated on the toilet?

10. Does voiding ever go on the seat, floor, or pants during toileting? This may indicate the need for a different toilet arrangement.

11. What level of toileting skill is acceptable? Institutional or school organization may prevent full toileting independence because doors are locked or staff are required to take a custodial role. Some parents also find it difficult to accept independent action from their handicapped offspring. Under these circumstances, it may be wise to concentrate on changing the expectations of parents and staff or changing the physical and administrative structure so that individuals are able to be independent. Occasionally, there may be justification for recommending training for less than full independence until these difficulties are overcome.

12. What drugs or other regular major treatments are being administered? Some drugs interfere with learning. In addition, it may be necessary to come to some agreement with the medical practitioner or other therapist about management of treatment during training.

13. What foods or activities are especially liked by the person? This information helps in choosing effective rewards to be used during training.

Check for Abnormalities or Disease

Usually, the major caregiver can provide most of the information about physical abnormalities or disease, and, occasionally, a medical examination will be required. The existence of any of the following problems may indicate that the person is unlikely to learn toileting skills with this programme. However, future training or different training procedures may be effective. The list that follows does not necessarily indicate that training is impossible.

In most cases of incontinence among handicapped persons, there are no signs of physical abnormality or disease. However, it is wise to check, as training may be not only expensive, but also distressing for a person who cannot achieve the training goals.

1. The person has poorly controlled epilepsy. A rough rule of thumb is five or more grand mal seizures a month during the past three months. Apart from the fact that epileptic seizures interrupt training for at least several hours, there is some evidence that the resulting neurological damage or disruption can prevent learning or destroy recent learning. Some disruption can also occur following petit mal seizures if they are frequent. In addition, severe epilepsy usually requires heavy regular doses of anticonvulsants. These often have side effects which also interfere with learning.

2. The person has a physical handicap that interferes significantly with hand use (e.g. hands unable to grasp and let go voluntarily).

3. The person has a physical handicap that interferes significantly with walking (e.g. cannot walk from bathroom door to toilet unsupported).
   (Note: These last two problems should be assessed carefully. Several children using walking aids, one child who could crawl and pull himself up to stand, and one child who only had the use of one hand, learned most of the toileting skills despite their disabilities. However, they were taught using programmes aimed at less than full independence. We have not trained any persons with severe physical disabilities using this programme.)

4. The person has a significant visual deficit (e.g. cannot see enough to recognize a familiar person).

5. The person has a significant hearing deficit (e.g. cannot hear normal speech). We have not trained anyone with severe sensory deficits using this programme. Several children whom we trained had some deficit but were able to hear the alarms. Additional procedures and modifications would be required to compensate for severe sensory deficit.

6. The person has chronic constipation or frequent diarrhoea. Often, these two problems are easily overcome with systematic behaviour or dietary changes (Bettison, 1978, 1979). Toilet training to independence is unlikely to be effective until these problems have been overcome.

7. The person has spinal-cord problems and possible neurogenic bladder. Toilet training in these cases is unlikely to be successful, although there are several reports of spina bifida children becoming partially or fully self-toileting as a result of systematic toilet training programmes.

8. The person has coeliac disease. This is often associated with loose bowel motions that are made worse by slight dietary changes. Until this has been brought under control, toilet training is unlikely to be effective.

Contract with the Major Caregivers

No matter how well a handicapped person may learn self-toileting skills, his performance of them is dependent on the social environment in which he lives. This is especially important immediately after training during the Maintenance Phase. The pattern of interaction and reinforcements that parents and staff provide can actively work against the learning and performance of independent toileting skills. Ideally, the major caregivers should work as co-trainers alongside the training staff. In many cases it has been one or both parents who have worked with us during training. We have found that working together in this way has developed mutual trust and confidence between trainers and parents. Trainers came to respect and provide positive support for the parents. Parents, on the other hand, lost the common feeling of hopelessness as they saw their offspring progress quickly through the programme. They began to see the strengths and abilities of both themselves and the handicapped person and developed new confidence and methods for teaching and handling problems. Furthermore, their involvement in the successful learning of the handicapped person gave them an understanding of the factors involved in self-toileting and considerable motivation to continue their effective work, both during and after the Maintenance Phase.

Parent involvement can be arranged through a formal contract between trainers and parents. This ensures that both know exactly what is expected and avoids misunderstanding or disruptions to training. Few parents can be involved full time. We have found that a minimum of two half-days a week has provided effective involvement for most parents. The contract should be simple and include the following:

1. The aim of the training programme.

2. The maximum length of time set aside for training.

3. The times and days each week during which the handicapped person is to attend.

4. The times and days each week during which the parents(s) act as co-trainers.

5. The contribution expected of the parent(s).

6. The contribution expected of the trainers in terms of teaching both the handicapped person and the parent(s).

7. Transport arrangements to get the handicapped person to and from training.

8. Any other arrangements, such as in the case of illness, both during training time and in the event of inability to attend.

9. The dates of any formal reviews of the programme.

10. Specified arrangements if progress ceases or the training aim is not reached within the maximum time alloted.

11. Agreement on how records, including videotape or film, may be used.

12. What should happen if either party breaks the agreement.

13. Agreement of parent(s) to carry out the Maintenance Phase and to keep in regular contact with the trainers during that phase.

14. Both parent(s) and trainer(s) should sign the contract once it has been agreed upon and both should have a copy.

The same benefits of co-training apply to institution staff, teachers, and other regular therapists, however, it is often more difficult to involve them in the same way. Teachers can rarely leave their classes, therapists usually have a heavy case load, and institution staff often do not stay in one living unit long enough to follow a programme through to completion. In general, the more involvement and knowledge these people have, the more effective they will be in assisting with the Maintenance Phase. Although teachers and other staff may not be involved in the training, it is wise to have written agreement from them to release the handicapped person from their programmes during training and to carry out the maintenance procedures after training. On occasion, we have also found it necessary to get the written agreement of the medical practitioner who treats the handicapped person. The agreement has been to leave current medication unchanged during training or, in the event of essential changes, to inform the trainers.

The Final Decision

At the end of this first assessment, you and the caregivers are in a position to decide whether the handicapped person should enter this programme. Training to independence is effective at any age. We have successfully trained four-year-olds and fifty-year-olds. However, circumstances and behaviour at all ages can change over time. Consequently, there should be no more than four weeks between this initial assessment and entry into the second assessment and training. If a person has to wait for longer before training is available, it is necessary to interview the caregiver(s) again, including another Balthazar Toileting Questionnaire, to ensure that this programme is still suitable.

Choosing the Training Environment

Many toilet-training programmes are, in fact, more effective when they take place in the normal environment. However, the majority of handicapped persons who we trained using this programme displayed a number of maladaptive responses in their normal environment. They also displayed considerable long-term difficulty or resistance to teaching in their normal environment. For these persons, complex and intensive training procedures were necessary, which required considerable control of both the physical and social environment. For these reasons we ran this programme in a special Intensive Training Unit, away from the normal living environment. This has proved to be beneficial in a number of ways. Many family toilets could not accommodate the equipment and trainers. Schools and residential units are often unable to provide a toilet which is not used by other people during the day. In addition, two experienced trainers can often train two or three persons at once with the help of parents. This would not be possible if each learner was trained in his or her own home. Moreover, both learners and parents have gained a great deal of support from other learners and parents in the programme at the same time. A small group of learners, parents, and trainers creates a social environment which provides appropriate models and further reinforcement for appropriate toileting behaviour and effective human interaction.

However, this programme does not require a special unit or a group to be effective. It can be carried out anywhere as long as the following conditions exist:

1. Privacy, away from frequent interruption.

2. One toilet for each learner.

3. All equipment readily available.

4. Safe storage for equipment during nontraining time.

5. Enough room to accommodate two or three people.

6. Easy and immediate access to expert advice and relief.

7. Easy control over the amount of space available during Phase 7 when the learner has increasing freedom to move away from the toilet.

8. Easy transport for the handicapped person or trainers, if training occurs away from their normal environment.

While several trainers and handicapped persons working together is often beneficial, the presence of other persons who are not fully involved in the programme and the interruptions caused by telephone calls or frequent visitors are disruptive.

Getting to Know Each Other

During the first few days of attendance before training begins, the second assessment is carried out. This stage provides three things. It allows the trainers to observe all voiding and toileting behaviour. At the same time, the handicapped person and the caregiver settle into the new environment and get to know the trainers. The caregiver has a chance to look through the manual and any other material related to the programme, as well as discuss the training and management procedures in detail. In addition, the trainers can observe any individual learning or behaviour problems and establish a range of effective reinforcers.

Environment

The learner is to remain in the activity area, including the toilet area, in which training will take place. Toys and activities should be provided that involve the learner, the caregiver, and the trainer. This area should be comfortable, pleasant, and big enough to accommodate a reasonable range of activities.

Clothing

The learner should be dresssed in normal clothes, with spare clothing available in case of voiding accidents.

Equipment and Materials

1. A range of play and recreation equipment that is suitable for the age and ability level of the handicapped person. Many trainers have shown considerable ingenuity in devising attractive activities with rugs, paper, boxes, etc.
2. One observation record sheet each day (*see* Appendix B).
3. Pen or pencil.
4. A variety of foods, toys, and activities to test as reinforcers.
5. Drinks, snacks, and lunch.
6. Comfortable chairs.
7. Table and chairs for quiet activities and meals.
8. Cloths, mop, and bucket.
9. Receptacles to hold soiled or wet clothing.
10. Washing and bathing facilities.

Observation of Voiding and Toileting

During the first few days of attendance before training begins, all voiding and toileting behaviour is observed and recorded on the observation record sheet (*see* Appendix B). The procedure is as follows:

Pants Checks

1. Every half hour the trainer checks the learner's pants. This should be done as unobtrusively as possible. You can often incorporate the pants check into a game if the learner is a child. However, sometimes accidents will be no more than a small patch on the pants. The pants check, therefore, needs to be more than a casual glance.
2. Record the pants check on the record sheet.
3. If the learner is discovered wet or soiled, quietly change his pants and wipe up any mess.

Record of Accidents

Record all voiding accidents on the record sheet in the space provided, even if they are discovered between pants checks. The record will include the time the accident was discovered, whether it was urine, faeces, or both, and the size of the accident.

Record of Toileting

If the learner goes towards the toilet without any direction, follow quietly and observe and record each toileting step in the space provided. Do not help the learner unless you are absolutely certain that he cannot perform that task himself. If you give any help, always use the least possible prompt or guidance first. Your aim is to observe the maximum level of skill that the learner has. The amount of help required is recorded for each task on the observation record sheet in the spaces provided. The following is a guide for testing the amount of help required. Start with Step 1. If the learner does not respond to this, move on to successive steps until the learner responds. The step at which he responds is what you enter on the record sheet.

Step 1. A point or gesture in the direction that the learner should move.

Step 2. Verbal instruction, such as "John, pants up".

Step 3. A little physical guidance, such as a touch or movement of the appropriate parts of the learner's body to start or finish the task.

Step 4. Physical guidance for approximately half the task.

Step 5. Physical guidance for approximately all of the task. (*see* the section on physical guidance in Chap. 4).

If, during the first observation day, the learner makes no approach to the toilet, direction may be provided on subsequent days. Only direct the learner approximately three times each day: at mid-morning, lunchtime, and mid-afternoon. The same principle applies to direction to go to the toilet as to all other tasks during the observation period. Use the least possible prompt or guidance first and only increase it step by step until a level of direction is reached to which the learner responds. The step at which the learner responds is what you enter on the record sheet.

How Long to Observe

Your aim during the observation period is to obtain a stable record, with no clear trend towards increasing skill on any of the tasks. Three days of observation with no trend to improvement is the minimum required. However, some handicapped persons may improve in performance of some or all tasks during the first few days of observation as they adjust to the new people and surroundings. Some also improve as a direct result of the independence in toileting allowed them during this period. If the person improves to accident-free self-toileting over three or more days, this programme is unnecessary, and he should be returned to his normal environment with a maintenance programme tailored to his particular needs and environment, as described in the section on unsatisfactory baseline record in

Chapter 6. The longest observation period we needed to obtain three days in a row with no improvement was ten days.

It is difficult to see whether there is any trend to improvement in the observation record. This is especially so if the learner's performance varies a great deal. However, you can see any trends at a glance on a graph of each task (*see* Appendix E). Variation up and down on the graph does not indicate improvement unless there is also a general trend upwards for all tasks and toilet use, or downwards for the size and number of accidents and time taken to void in the toilet.

Selecting Effective Rewards

During the first few days of the observation period, you should select some educational or recreation activities that the learner has not fully mastered. Present these during several sessions each day. Sessions should last from ten to thirty minutes, depending on the nature of the activity and the concentration span of the learner. During these sessions you can try a number of foods, toys, and activities for their effectiveness as rewards. This is not intended to be a formal, well-documented programme. However, you will need to record the range of items that the learner works hard to obtain. These will be the rewards that you will use during training.

Occasionally, an individual is so strongly attracted to one object, food, or activity that its strength as a reward is relatively constant. However, most people quickly tire of a highly preferred reward after a number of presentations. Therefore, it is necessary to have a range of rewards from which the learner can choose or which you can choose if the learner is incapable of making a choice. The general procedure for testing rewards is as follows:

1. Set up the activity, paper and pen, and test rewards so that you can reach them easily.

2. Direct the learner to the activity, using the minimum prompting and guidance necessary.

3. Praise the learner immediately upon task completion and present the first reward.

4. Do this a number of times until you are sure that either:
   a. the learner is not interested in the reward;
   b. he does not try to perform the task in order to get the reward; or
   c. he is trying to perform the task in order to get the reward.

5. If the learner tries to perform in order to have the reward, you can record that as a possible reinforcer.

6. Follow the same procedure with the other test rewards.

If you find that none or only one or two of the test rewards are effective, you may have to use some ingenuity in searching for other possible rewards. Observe the choices the person makes during free activities, and ask further questions of the caregivers about preferred activities and behaviours. An object or activity is only rewarding if it increases the likelihood of behaviour that it follows, and things that are rewarding are often highly specific to the individual. Some of the rewards that we have found to be effective with individual learners have been unusual, for instance: tearing paper, being wrapped in a rug, being stroked, or playing with a piece of string.

Planning for Behaviour Management

During the pretraining stage, many of the problem behaviours that require management are likely to show up. This allows the trainers to develop consistent management techniques before training begins. Many of the problems that we met are described in Chapter 6. During the testing of this programme, the pretraining period allowed the trainers and caregivers to discuss and try new management procedures before the work of training actually began. This was especially important if the handicapped person or the caregiver consistently displayed inappropriate responses. We only used procedures, such as time-out, after we were sure that the caregiver understood and accepted them. Many caregivers had developed very effective management procedures. The period before training allowed both the caregiver and the trainers to show each other and practice together their most effective procedures. It is important for trainers to remember that parents know their children very well and usually have many skills to impart.

Chapter 4
OUTLINE OF THE PROGRAMME

WHAT DOES THIS PROGRAMME TEACH?

THIS PROGRAMME is designed to teach all the steps involved in fully independent self-toileting. It has been arranged so that the learner is always able to complete the tasks successfully and experience the satisfaction that this brings. To enable this, toileting has been broken down into small steps so that only a few tasks are taught at a time. The last step is learned first. Once this is performed independently and smoothly, the second last step is added to the task, and so on. This enables the learner to gradually build up the toileting sequence as a smooth performance. At the same time as each new step is added, the learner also has plenty of chance to practice the previously learned steps.

This learning process is very important for those handicapped persons who have difficulty in learning and performing complex sequences of skills. It helps focus their attention on each of the cues, which tells them which skill is required. It gives them a great deal of practice in recognising these cues and in carrying out the appropriate movements, it builds their confidence so that they no longer look for guidance and direction, and it enables them to experience the pleasure that comes from independent achievement.

The training is divided into seven phases. Each phase teaches one or more of the skills involved in self-toileting. At the same time, a number of other skills are taught that are useful, not only in independent toileting, but also in learning and performing other tasks. Many of the children who have been trained with this programme have learned to pay more attention to instructions, to give more concentration to a task while ignoring other distractions, to sit willingly for periods of time, to take the initiative in a variety of situations, and to persevere in solving simple, everyday problems themselves.

The use of toilet tissue, flushing the toilet, and hand washing after toileting is complete are not taught in this programme. We did not see this as essential to the processes of bladder and bowel control, although they are clearly important for hygiene. These are skills that require finer motor control and judgment than pulling pants up and down and as such would take considerable time to teach. Each would need a separate phase to incorporate it into the toileting sequence, and each phase would considerably increase the time needed to complete the programme. Most persons for whom this programme is suitable have serious learning problems, which could make the learning of such complex skills extremely difficult. However, they may be able to learn them and insert them into the toileting sequence at a later date once basic self-toileting is well established and habitual. If you consider that an individual could cope with these tasks and would benefit from learning them during the programme, you would need to analyse each task carefully and design new phases to teach them. These could be inserted into the appropriate sections of the programme. The major problem to consider in these cases is the effectiveness of the reward when it is separated from actual toilet use by two additional tasks.

The Phases

Phase 1

The primary aim of this phase is to teach the procedure for pulling up underpants without help. It also begins the process of teaching the learner to pay attention and concentrate. Consequently, this phase is useful even for those who are already fairly proficient at pulling up pants. In addition this phase establishes the trainer as someone whom the learner likes and wishes to please. Finally, this phase helps the learner feel comfortable with routine practice sessions before the most intensive part of the programme is introduced.

Phase 2

This phase teaches standing from the toilet and immediately pulling up pants as one smooth action. Many people who have been trained with this programme could already get themselves off the toilet, but did not move straight away to pull their pants up. The joining of these tasks is as important as the separate performance of each task.

Phase 3

This phase teaches several skills. It begins to teach the learner to recognize the cues that signal bladder or bowel tension. At the same time, it teaches how to tighten the perineal muscles and stop the flow should voiding begin away from the toilet. It also teaches sitting quietly on the toilet in the best position so that voluntary relaxation of the sphincter can occur. Finally, it teaches the learner to wait until voiding is complete before standing.

Phase 4

This phase concentrates on two additional skills. First, it teaches the holding back of voiding for a little longer. At the same time, the learner practices seating himself in the correct position for voiding in the toilet. Sitting on the toilet rather than standing is taught. This ensures that self-toileting is learned for both bowel movements and urination. It also avoids the difficulty that some handicapped men and boys have in aiming urine while standing so that it does not splash on the seat, floor, or clothing.

Phase 5

This phase requires the learner to hold back voiding for even longer while he pulls down pants before sitting on the toilet. Once this phase is complete, the learner can perform the essential toileting sequence smoothly.

Phase 6

This phase helps the learner who is still relying on direction from others to move towards the toilet and to gradually take more initiative in deciding to go to the toilet alone.

Phase 7

The learner only progresses to this phase when he is going to the toilet alone, voiding, and performing all the other tasks smoothly and competently without accidents. During this phase, the learner practises going to the toilet from increasing distances and with increasingly more distractions until he is interrupting normal activities to go to the toilet alone.

Maintenance Phase

During this phase, the learner goes back into normal school, work, and home activities. He learns to use his independent toileting skills in the presence of many other people and in the whole range of situations and environments that are part of his normal life.

Who Can Train?

Although in theory any one who is committed to helping handicapped persons to independence can use this programme, there are certain personal skills and attitudes as well as working conditions that will maximise your chance of success. The aim of this programme is to provide a positive and successful learning experience. You should not try to use this programme unless you can be reasonably sure that you can achieve this.

When beginning to use this programme, you should start by working with only one learner at a time. You should begin with handicapped persons who already have a number of toileting skills and who present few management problems. In this way you will be able to practise the procedures without the complications that may arise when a learner has a number of problems. It will also maximise your chances of success and give you the confidence to handle more complex problems. In addition, success from the beginning will ensure that others feel positive about the programme and provide you with the necessary support.

Once you have successfully trained several handicapped persons, you may consider working with more than one learner at a time or teaching other trainers to use the programme. However, this is a programme that requires one-to-one teaching most of the time. We only advise the training of several persons together if your staffing allows one trainer for each learner during all phases.

Necessary Work Conditions

1. Your close colleagues and superiors should be fully committed to your using the programme and carrying it through to completion, including the regular supervision of the maintenance phase and follow-up.

2. You should have uninterrupted use of a toilet and bathroom area.

3. You should have free access to the equipment, materials, and facilities required for the programme.

4. You should have ready access to medical and other resources required for the initial assessment.

5. There should be at least two of you available and equally committed, so that you can relieve each other during the programme. This ensures that the programme continues, while making allowance for meal times, illness, and the need for relief from what can sometimes be stressful or arduous work.

6. You should have ready access for advice to at least one person who is experienced in both caring for handicapped people and using behavioural training methods.

Necessary Personal Skills and Attitudes

1. You should feel confident and comfortable with systematic training and recordkeeping.

2. You need to be patient, gentle, and firm.

3. You should respect and care for handicapped people.

4. At least one of you should have some basic knowledge of and experience with behavioural methods.

5. It is tiring to concentrate on training. Even when you are relaxed and confident, you still have to remain constantly alert and paying close attention to the procedures. Therefore, you need to be thorough and painstaking.

Training Time

The shortest time to success, excluding the Maintenance Phase, for any child has been approximately three weeks. Many handicapped persons will take two months or more. Similarly, the Maintenance Phase can vary considerably, and it can take from three weeks to six months or more. The length of this phase will depend partly on the ability of the learner and partly on the consistency and reliability of the people carrying it out.

We have usually worked with children during normal school hours from 9:00 a.m. to 3:30 p.m. on weekdays. This provides an adequate block of time for the learner to consolidate the skills, but does not disrupt normal home life. The break from training over the weekend does not appear to disrupt learning.

Main Procedures

Prompts

Initially, the learner needs to be told what to do. These instructions are given only once, are as simple as possible, and always the same. They consist of:

- The person's name
- A one- or two-word instruction
- A gesture
- A touch

This is a prompt. It uses three sensory modalities: hearing, sight and touch. This increases the likelihood that the learner will understand your instructions.

The use of prompts achieves two things:

1. It ensures that the directions are consistent. The learner is, therefore, given every chance to learn the meaning of the directions and the likelihood of confusion is reduced.

2. It ensures that directions are only given once. This helps the learner to pay attention immediately and avoids the confusion and resentment that often occurs when people constantly talk while the learner is trying to concentrate. Repeated instructions often teach a person that he does not have to do what is asked until the instruction has been given a number of times.

Fading of Prompts

The prompts are gradually reduced for each task until the learner can perform it without any direction. This helps the learner to gradually take the initiative and prevents fear, lack of confidence, and resistance from interfering with learning.

The fading of prompts is always carried out in the same way. One part of the prompt at a time is left out as soon as performance is perfect on several occasions.

The prompts are faded in the following order:

1. The touch is left out.

2. The person's name is left out.

3. One word of the instruction at a time is left out.

4. The gesture is made smaller (finger movements instead of a full-hand movement).

5. The hands are held ready to give the prompt, but no gesture is given.

6. No prompt is given.

Physical Guidance

Many handicapped persons do not know how to move to achieve a given result. They do not explore and try things voluntarily and so do not build up a range of skills that they can adapt to new tasks. Physical guidance allows the trainer to move the learner through the performance so that he is practising the movements, even though he may not be able to initiate them himself. It also ensures that the child who resists doing things when asked, gradually relaxes and accepts the task as something that is part of his daily life.

Physical guidance enables the trainer to ensure that the learner does what is asked without feeling frustrated or angry. It also helps the trainer to observe the learner closely. In this way the trainer gains the detailed understanding of the learner, which is crucial in making the programme a real teaching and learning experience for both.

If the learner does not immediately start the correct movement after the prompt is given or stops partway through, give gentle, physical guidance. With your hands, move the appropriate parts of the learner's body through the required motions. Your aim is always to give as little guidance as possible in order to give the learner every opportunity to make the movements alone. Therefore, you should be ready to release control the second the learner begins to make the right movement. You can only sense this initiative on the learner's part if your touch or grasp is light, slow, and gentle. However, when you withdraw your control, your hands should be kept close to the learner, shadowing his movement in order to give immediate guidance should his movements stop or go in the wrong direction. If the learner begins to move in the wrong direction or pull away, you should block the movement. Do not force the learner in the right direction. Block the incorrect movement so that the learner is still, until he relaxes and you can continue the guidance without resistance.

Your aim is also to reduce your guidance until it is no longer needed. You may begin with a gentle grasp and guidance for the total movement. You should reduce this as quickly as possible over trials to a gentle push and then just a touch. Watch and feel the learner's movements carefully, so that you can reduce or take away guidance the instant he takes the initiative. As the learner moves more confidently, you should keep your hands close by. Once you feel sure that he will always carry out the correct movements, you can relax and merely observe.

Physical guidance is crucial to the success of the programme. It allows you to show the learner what to do without force; it reduces the likelihood of resistance or fear; it enables the learner to develop confidence; it prevents the trainer from confusing the learner with constant talking; and enables both the trainer and learner to concentrate solely on the task at hand.

Extra Fluids

Once voiding in the toilet is required during Phase 3, the learner is offered drinks every half hour. Some handicapped persons will drink as much as you give them. We have found that more than an average of one or two cups of fluid every half hour causes discomfort and can also lead to vomiting. Less than half to one cup every half hour does not build up sufficient fluid in the bladder, and voiding is infrequent. The aim of the extra fluid intake is to induce frequent voiding so that the learner has plenty of practise in carrying out the toileting tasks. The extra fluids also appear to increase bladder capacity so that the learner eventually voids only about seven times a day. This is the usual average frequency for most people who are eight years or older.

Providing a variety of drinks that allows a choice of tastes will often persuade the learner to drink. Do not force drinking. Use gentle encouragement, games, and praise to encourage drinking if the child is reluctant. Some handicapped persons are unable to drink without spilling. Use a cloth or feeder to protect the learner's clothing and gentle guidance to teach self-control of the cup. Learning independence in this skill increases the learner's confidence in general.

Reward

Many handicapped persons are unused to experiencing the satisfaction of trying something new and being successful; consequently, they are often unwilling to try. Reward during training provides an additional incentive to try. Two forms of reward are given together after the successful completion of each trial.

1. *Praise and affection.* This should be given with real meaning and enthusiasm and should be in a form that is acceptable to the learner. A bland "good boy" is not reward in itself. It does not stand out from the rest of your verbal statements. Some handicapped persons will accept a bear hug, some feel more comfortable with a companionable pat on the shoulder, some like effusive praise, and others prefer very private and personal praise. No matter how you give your praise and affection, it must be sincere and enthusiastic.

2. *Some tangible activity, food, or article.* This needs to be something that the learner will make a considerable effort to obtain. Individual persons will seek different things. Some will work for small pieces of special foods such as chips, sultanas, fruit, or ice cream. Try to avoid sweets if possible, but some will only work for sweets. Other handicapped persons will work in order to look at a book, listen to music, play with a piece of string or doll, or tear a piece of paper. This reward must be something that can be provided immediately in the confines of the bathroom.

Some handicapped persons do not notice much about other people, so that praise and affection are not rewarding for them. The consistent pairing of this with the tangible reward usually ensures that praise and affection alone do become rewarding. This is important for the later Maintenance Phase, as well as for the later learning of other tasks. Many human skills are acquired through the approval of other people.

Fading of Reward

The programme is designed so that rewards gradually become less frequent. During the first two phases, the learner is rewarded three times every half hour. During Phase 3, reward only follows successful voiding in the toilet and is, therefore, less frequent. As the learner begins to hold urine for longer periods, and once the extra fluids cease, toileting becomes less frequent so that rewards may only be given two or three times a day. During the final Maintenance Phase only praise and affection are given. These gradually drop out as the learner becomes more independent and the trainers miss seeing some toiletings. Finally, the learner is toileting independently with little or no reward. This gradual fading of reward is important in helping the learner become self-motivated.

Recording

It is vital to the success of the programme that you record each procedure that you use and each performance of the learner. Sample record sheets are included in Appendix B at the back of this manual.

1. Because this programme is complex and includes a number of different procedures, keeping a continuous record of them is the only way you have of ensuring that your training is consistent and that you are following the programme.

2. Continuous recordkeeping enables several trainers to share the work of training while maintaining consistency.

3. Continuous recordkeeping enables you to see small changes in the learner's performance. Without records the complexity of the programme may prevent you from recognising when there are small improvements or when problems arise that you should do something about.

4. Continuous records are very important in giving you, as the trainer, immediate feedback about the success of your training. You are working as hard as the learner and also need some reward for your work. The learner's improvement and others' recognition of your work provides that reward.

5. Whenever you or the learner does something that you wish to remember, write a brief description on the record sheet. In this way, you can use your experience with that learner to help you with future handicapped persons who may display similar behaviour. You will find some of the common problems that we experienced and what we did about them in Chapter 6.

Chapter 5
HOW TO TRAIN

THIS CHAPTER describes in detail the procedures that you will use once a handicapped person has been assessed as ready for toilet training to independence. The first two phases of training are different from all the following phases, in that they do not require any systematic methods for dealing with voiding.

REQUIREMENTS FOR PHASES 1 AND 2

Environment

The learner is to remain in a play area close to the toilet. Toys and activities should be provided that involve both you and the learner. This helps build a pleasant relationship between you, so that both find it reinforcing to work together.

Trials are carried out by the toilet. During the remaining time, the learner is free to join in other activities.

Clothing

The learner is dressed in a top and underpants, which should not be too tight. Underpants that come to the waist are easier to handle than tight hipsters or briefs. Long shirts or dresses can be pinned up at the back to keep them out of the way during practise trials.

Equipment and Materials

1. One record sheet each day for the appropriate phase.
2. Pen or pencil.
3. A variety of rewards that have been determined as suitable during the Assessment Phase. These are positioned close to the toilet so that they can be offered immediately after a trial has been completed.
4. Tissues.
5. Cloths for protecting clothing and wiping up.
6. Mop and bucket.
7. A place to store wet and soiled pants.
8. Several changes of clothing for the learner.
9. Toys that can be played with between trials.

Structure of Trials

The learner has *three* practise trials every half hour. This is the optimum number of trials that give frequent enough practise without leading to boredom or stress during learning.

Going into the Toilet

Each half hour during the day, the learner accompanies you into the toilet area. Give as little direction as possible. It is better to say to the learner, "Come on, John," gesture towards the toilet, and then follow him or her in, rather than physically leading the person. The more independence you expect in every task, the more initiative the learner will display in toileting.

The Correct Position for Trials

The learner stands about one to two feet in front of the toilet seat and facing out into the room. This position should prevent the learner from trying to sit on the toilet. You stand or squat in front of and facing the learner. Use your hands to guide the learner so that he or she is standing still and does not sit or play around. Do not talk while you are getting him or her into position.

Getting the Learner's Attention

Use gentle guidance to get the learner's attention. He or she should be standing still and looking at you. You may need to gently guide his or her face. Wait until you have the learner's attention before giving the prompt. Do not talk while you are getting the learner's attention.

Rewards

Rewards always consist of affection and praise, immediately followed by the tangible reward. Because you are using prompts and guidance, the tasks you are teaching are always completed during Phases 1 and 2. Consequently, the learner is rewarded on each trial. No matter which task you are teaching, reward always follows immediately after the pants are pulled up all round. This helps the learner join the tasks together in sequence. The reward is always given in the toilet where the task is accomplished. You should stand in a position that prevents the learner from walking out of the toilet until you have given the reward. This helps tie the toileting tasks to the toilet area and reduces the likelihood that they will be performed in other inappropriate places.

Recording

There is a separate record sheet for each day (*see* Appendix B). In addition, there are specific record sheets for each phase. Each sheet has brief instructions and a number of labelled positions where you can mark in the step and prompt used, the time of trials, and the amount of guidance needed on each trial. Although there are no special procedures for dealing with toileting and accidents during Phases 1 and 2, there are spaces to mark in the time of toiletings and whether voiding occurred, as well as the time and size of accidents.

Each day, the date and the names of the learner and trainers are written on the record sheet. There is also some space on the record sheets for noting special events that you may wish to record.

Record each trial as soon as it is finished. Do not leave this until later, as you are likely to forget. Keep constantly looking over the record so that you can monitor progress and pick up any problems quickly.

Phase 1

Toileting Aim

The learner pulls up underpants from the knee to the waist without prompts or guidance, while standing with back to the toilet, on nine trials in a row. In this run of nine perfect trials, you may accept *no more* than two performances which require guidance.

Position of Pants

When the learner is in position, pull the pants down to the required position. If, during your preliminary assessment, the learner has not pulled his or her pants up from the knee or calf without instruction or guidance on 100 percent of the observed toiletings, begin at position 1.

Position 1. Pants positioned with the waistband on the hip and slightly above the curve of the buttocks.

Position 2. Pants positioned with the waistband just under the curve of the buttocks.

Position 3. Pants positioned with the waistband halfway down the thighs.

Position 4. Pants positioned with the waistband below the knees. If, during your preliminary assessment, the learner pulled the pants up from the knee or calf without instruction or guidance on 100 percent of the observed toiletings, begin at Position 4.

The Prompt

Give the following prompt clearly: "John, pants up," raise both hands to indicate up, and then touch the learner's hands. This is Prompt 1. Only give the prompt once. Do not say anything else until the task is completed.

Physical Guidance

If the learner does not immediately grasp the pants waistband, gently guide his or her hands so that the thumbs are inside the front of the pants waistband and the fingers are grasping the cloth. If necessary, use physical guidance to gently slide the hands into a position that will enable him or her to pull the pants up all round. The learner may have to have several pulls to get the pants up completely.

When to Start a New Pants Position

Continue the pants up trials at Position 1, until the learner has achieved three perfect performances in a row without guidance. Move to the next pants position, still using Prompt 1, until again three perfect performances in a row without guidance are achieved. Continue in this way until three perfect performances in a row, without guidance, are achieved in response to Prompt 1 at Position 4.

When to Start a New Prompt

Once this is achieved, move to Prompt 2. Each time a new prompt is used, the learner is likely to need some guidance again. This is especially so if the learner lacks confidence and looks to others to tell him or her what to do. Only move on to the next prompt when three perfect performances without guidance in a row are achieved. There are eight steps necessary to fade prompting, the eighth being the absence of a prompt. For the eighth prompt, take the learner into the toilet and pull his or her pants down to the knee. Then say and do nothing else, unless you need to give guidance.

When to Proceed to Phase 2

You can begin Phase 2 when the learner has pulled the pants up from the knee on at least seven out of nine trials in a row without any guidance from you, as soon as the pants are felt at knee level at Prompt 8.

Phase 2

Toileting Aim

The learner stands up from a sitting position on the toilet and pulls underpants up from the knee to the waist without prompts or guidance, on nine trials in a row. In this run of nine perfect trials, you may accept *no more* than two performances that require guidance.

The Correct Position

During this phase, you pull the learner's pants down to knee level and gently seat him or her on the toilet.

The Prompt

Once you have the learner's attention, give the following prompt clearly: "John, stand," raise both hands to indicate up, and then touch the learner's shoulders. This is Prompt 1. Only give the prompt once. Do not say anything else until the task is completed.

Physical Guidance

If the learner does not stand immediately, gently guide his or her body forward and up. Many handicapped persons at the beginning of Phase 2 may not realise that they should continue on to pull up their pants once they are standing. You may need to give minimal guidance for the first few trials until pulling up pants follows smoothly after standing.

When to Start a New Prompt

Continue to use Prompt 1 until the learner has stood up from the toilet following the prompt three times in a row without guidance, then move on to the next prompt. Only move to a new prompt after three performances in a row with no guidance at the previous prompt. There are seven steps necessary to fade prompting, the seventh being the absence of a prompt. For the seventh prompt, seat the learner on the toilet. Say and do nothing else unless you need to give guidance.

When to Proceed to Phase 3

You may begin Phase 3 when the learner has stood up from the toilet within seconds of being seated and pulled the pants up from the knee on at least seven out of nine trials in a row at Prompt 7 without any guidance from you.

REQUIREMENTS FOR PHASES 3 TO 7

Environment

The learner is to sit on a chair approximately two feet away from the toilet seat. Toys and activities should be provided that can be used in this position. Although you need not insist on constant sitting, it is important that the learner mostly remains on the chair. You will need to allow him or her to leave the chair in case toileting is intended. You can arrange a small table or chair, containing toys and books, next to the learner so that he or she can easily select things to do. This position keeps the toilet constantly in view as a reminder to the learner. In addition, it increases the ability of many persons to sit quietly and pay attention to what they are doing.

Clothing

This should be the same as for the first two phases. In addition, the learner should wear training pants with studs and a pants alarm attached (*see* Appendix A).

Equipment and Materials

In addition to the equipment and materials required for Phases 1 and 2 as described in this chapter, you will also need the following:

1. A variety of drinks that the child likes.

2. Several drinking mugs.

3. Approximately sixteen training pants with studs.

4. Washing and drying facilities close by. The training pants should not be sent to central laundries, as they are too rough on the studs.

5. A bowl or pot with studs that fits snugly in the toilet under the seat.

6. Two pants' alarms and leads plus one or two spare leads.

7. Two toilet alarms and leads.

8. Several spare batteries for the alarms.

9. Adhesive tape.

10. Scissors.

Before training begins each day, check that the pants and toilet alarms are working and that you have all the equipment and materials within easy reach. The pants and toilet alarms are described in Appendix A at the back of this manual. It helps if you or someone close by can use a screwdriver and soldering iron to make simple repairs to the alarms. Occasionally, a lead breaks, batteries need replacing, or components in the alarm become disconnected. Repairs are easy and do not require special knowledge. If you have no one who can make these repairs, you should have several spare alarms so that training is not held up while you send a malfunctioning alarm away for repair.

Structure of Trials

During these five phases, trials only occur in the two following situations:

1. When the learner has an accident and the pants alarm sounds.
2. When the learner goes to the toilet alone, carries out all the tasks perfectly, and voids in the toilet.

Extra Fluids

Every half hour offer drinks to the learner, and record how much is drunk. Extra fluids are offered throughout until Step 8 in Phase 7. The last two drinks that you offer each day should be small. This prevents the learner from going home with a full bladder. Generally, only offer half a cup of drink at 2:30 p.m. and a quarter of a cup at 3:00 p.m.

Rewards

Continue giving the rewards in exactly the same way as during Phases 1 and 2. The rewards are given once the learner has voided in the toilet, stood up, and pulled pants up all round. Do *not* give the rewards if no voiding occurs in the toilet. Continue to keep the learner in the toilet area until the pants are fully up.

Recording

Record sheets are marked in the same way as during Phases 1 and 2. However, when recording toileting, the time the learner is seated on the toilet and the time when voiding in the toilet actually begins are both recorded. This is especially useful for those handicapped persons who begin by being unable to reliably relax the perineal muscles at will. It will show you if this skill is being learned.

Self-Toileting

If the learner walks into the toilet, pulls down pants, voids, stands when finished, and pulls up pants, treat it as a successful trial. Record it as an SI (self-initiation), and give the reward immediately after the pants are up all round. Do not count self-initiated toiletings among the successful trials required before progressing to the next phase. However, if the learner successfully toilets him or herself without accidents on at least eight out of ten voidings in a row, omit the remaining phases and go straight on to Phase 7.

Phase 3

Toileting Aim

The learner sits quietly in the appropriate position after being placed on the toilet, urinates and/or defecates in the toilet, and stands when finished without guidance on ten voidings in a row. In this run of ten perfect trials, you may accept *no more* than two performances with no voiding or which require guidance for remaining seated.

When the Pants Alarm Sounds

1. Immediately upon hearing the pants alarm, say "no" loudly and sharply. Do not say anything else until toileting is completed.

2. Quickly take the learner to the toilet, pull his or her pants down to the knees, and seat in the correct position for voiding, then wait for voiding to occur. Note the time that the learner was seated.

3. Sometimes the pants alarm does not sound immediately when voiding begins. This can happen if the alarm is flooded or if the stream does not reach the studs in the pants. Because you are close to the learner, you will usually see the urine on the pants or chair. You should say "no" loudly and take the learner to the toilet as if the pants alarm had sounded.

4. Sometimes the pants alarm sounds and you cannot see any sign of urination on the pants. You should still carry out the procedure. Do not spend time checking the pants for dampness or soiling. The pants' alarms are sensitive and will sound with only one or two drops of moisture on the studs.

Physical Guidance

Sit or stand close enough to the learner to give guidance if he or she does not sit quietly until voiding is complete. Use guidance to ensure that the learner does not stand until voiding is completely finished. Remember that activity can often prevent the learner from relaxing, and thus voiding cannot occur. Many handicapped persons at the beginning of Phase 3 may not realize that they should stand and pull up their pants once voiding has finished. You may need to give minimal guidance for the first few trials until these tasks follow smoothly after voiding.

How Long Should the Learner Sit on the Toilet?

The learner should remain sitting quietly on the toilet until voiding is complete. Note the time that voiding begins. If the learner does not void immediately, he or she should remain seated either until voiding occurs or for twenty minutes, whichever is the shortest. If voiding has not occurred by the end of twenty minutes, give the minimum amount of guidance necessary to get him or her to stand and pull the pants up.

Reward

Once the learner has voided, stood up, and pulled up the pants all round, you should immediately give the reward. If voiding does not occur, but instead the learner sits for twenty minutes, do not give any reward. Do not allow the learner out of the toilet area until the pants are completely up.

Other Tasks for the Trainer

1. Once the learner has been seated on the toilet, unclip the pants alarm leads from the studs in the pants so that the alarm stops sounding.

2. Once voiding is complete, gently take the wet or soiled pants off the learner and put on clean pants, with a pants alarm attached, to knee level.

3. After the learner has stood up from the toilet, you may need to wipe him or her before allowing the pants to be pulled up. Do this as quickly as possible.

4. Before allowing the learner to sit back on the chair, you may need to wipe the chair or floor.

5. Once the learner is back on the chair, empty the bowl in the toilet, clean it, and place it back in position with the leads attached ready for the next toileting.

When to Proceed to Phase 4

Once at least eight out of ten toiletings in a row have resulted in voiding with no guidance to remain seated in the appropriate position, move on to Phase 4.

Phase 4

Toileting Aim

The learner seats him or herself in the appropriate position after being taken to the toilet and having pants pulled down, urinates and/or defecates in the toilet, without prompts or guidance, on ten voidings in a row. In this run of ten perfect trials, you may accept *no more* than two performances with no voiding or which require guidance for sitting.

Procedure

The initial procedures are exactly the same as for Phase 3, except that when you have pulled the learner's pants down to knee level, make sure that you have his or her attention.

The Prompt

Give the following prompt clearly: "John, sit," lower both hands to indicate down, and then touch the learner's shoulders. This is Prompt 1. Only give the prompt once. Do not say anything else until toileting is completed.

Physical Guidance

If the learner does not sit immediately, gently guide his or her body back and down. Some handicapped persons may not be able to position themselves appropriately while sitting. You may need to move your guidance to hip level to ensure that the position taken is correct. The best position will vary for different learners. You may also need to give minimal guidance for remaining seated, standing, and pulling up pants during the first few trials in this new phase.

When to Start a New Prompt

Continue to use Prompt 1 until the learner has sat on the toilet in the appropriate position three times in a row without guidance, then move on to the next prompt. Move on to each new prompt after three performances in a row with no guidance at the previous prompt. There are seven steps necessary to fade prompting, the seventh being the absence of a prompt. For the seventh prompt, pull the learner's pants down to the knee and then say and do nothing else unless you need to give guidance.

When to Proceed to Phase 5

Once the learner has seated him or herself in the appropriate position without prompting or guidance and voided in the toilet on at least eight out of ten voidings, you may move on to Phase 5.

Phase 5

Toileting Aim

The learner pulls down pants after being taken quickly into the toilet, seats him or herself in the appropriate position, and urinates and/or defecates in the toilet without prompts or guidance on ten voidings in a row. In this run of ten perfect trials, you may accept *no more* than two performances with no voiding or which require guidance for pants down.

Procedure

The initial procedure is exactly the same as for Phase 3, except that when you have quickly taken the learner into the toilet and positioned him or her with back to the toilet, pull the pants down to the required position.

Position of Pants

If, during your preliminary assessment, the learner has *not* pulled the pants down from the waist without instruction or guidance on 100 percent of the observed toiletings, begin at Position 1.

Position 1. Pants positioned with waistband halfway down the thighs.

Position 2. Pants positioned with the waistband just under the curve of the buttocks.

Position 3. Pants positioned with waistband on the hip and slightly above the curve of the buttocks.

Position 4. Pants positioned with the waistband, on the waist. If, during your preliminary assessment, the learner pulled the pants down from the waist to knee or calf level without instruction or guidance on 100 percent of the observed toiletings, begin at Position 4.

The Prompt

Once you have the learner's attention, give the following prompt clearly: "John, pants down," lower both hands to indicate down, and then touch the learner's hands. This is Prompt 1. Only give the prompt once. Do not say anything else until toileting is completed.

Physical Guidance

If the learner does not immediately grasp the pants waistband, gently guide his or her hands so that the thumbs are inside the front of the pants. If necessary, use physical guidance to gently slide the hands into a position that will enable the pants to be pushed down. Use guidance to prevent the pants being taken further than the knees. Some handicapped persons may not realize, to begin with, that they should go on to sit. You may need to give minimal guidance for the first few trials until sitting follows smoothly after pulling down the pants.

When to Start a New Pants Position

Continue at Position 1 for all toiletings until the learner has achieved three pants-down performances in a row without guidance. Move to the next pants position until again three perfect performances without guidance are achieved. Continue in this way until three perfect pants-down performances in a row are achieved without guidance at Position 4.

When to Start a New Prompt

Once this is achieved, move to Prompt 2. Each time you start a new prompt, the learner may need guidance. Only move onto the next prompt when three perfect pants-down performances in a row are achieved without guidance. There are eight steps necessary to fade prompting, the eighth being the absence of a prompt. For the eighth prompt, you should quickly take the learner into the toilet after saying, "no" loudly and clearly; then you should not say or do anything else unless you need to give guidance.

When to Proceed to Phase 6

Once the learner has pulled down pants from the waist to the knee and sat and voided in the toilet without prompting or guidance on at least eight out of ten voidings, you may move on to Phase 6.

Phase 6

Toileting Aim

The learner performs the whole toileting sequence as well as urinates and/or defecates in the toilet without having an accident and without prompts or guidance on ten voidings in a row. In this run of ten perfect trials, you may accept *no more* than two performances with either accidents or no voidings or which require guidance for toilet approach.

Procedure

The initial procedure is exactly the same as for Phase 3, except that when you have said "no" loudly and sharply, you do not take the learner into the toilet. If he or she gets up and walks to the toilet alone, do not interfere.

The Prompt

Give the following prompt clearly: "John, toilet," point to the toilet with arm fully extended, and then touch the learner's back. This is Prompt 1. Only give the prompt once. Do not say anything else until toileting is completed.

Physical Guidance

If the learner does not immediately stand and move towards the toilet, use physical guidance. You may need to give minimal guidance for the first few toiletings until pants down follows smoothly after the learner reaches the toilet.

When to Start a New Prompt

Continue with Prompt 1 at every toileting until the learner has got up from the chair and walked to the toilet without guidance three times in a row. Once this is achieved, move to the next prompt. Each time a new prompt is used, the learner may need some guidance again. Only move to the next prompt after three toilet approaches in a row have been achieved without guidance. There are seven steps necessary to fade prompting, the seventh being the absence of a prompt. The seventh prompt requires you to do or say nothing after saying "no" unless you need to give guidance.

When to Proceed to Phase 7

Once the learner has performed the whole toileting sequence, including voiding in the toilet, without accidents, prompts, or guidance on at least eight out of ten voidings, you may move on to Phase 7.

Phase 7

Toileting Aim

The learner independently toilets him or herself from anywhere in the activity area, without prompting or guidance, without alarms or extra drinks, and while dressed in normal clothes, on ten voidings in a row. In this run of ten perfect toiletings, you may accept *no more* than two toiletings with either accidents or no voiding or which require guidance for any part of the toileting sequence.

Procedure

You are now mainly observing and recording the learner's toileting. However, you will continue to offer drinks every half hour. You will still say "no" loudly and sharply if the pants alarm sounds. In addition, you will still give affection and praise, immediately followed by the tangible reward, as soon as the pants are up all round. For this reason, you will always need to follow the learner at a distance when he or she goes to the toilet. If toilet approach does not follow the pants alarm sounding, use minimal guidance.

The Steps Toward Full Independent Toileting

You will begin this phase with the learner still seated on a chair about two feet from the toilet. Once he or she has successfully gone to the toilet alone from this position without accidents for three voidings in a row, move on to the next step. There are eight steps altogether. Each time you start a new step, the learner may have an occasional accident for the first few voidings. Only move on to the next step after three successful self-toiletings in a row without accidents (Steps 1 to 6). Remain at both Steps 7 and 8 until there are eight out of ten successful self-toiletings in a row without accidents.

The steps are as follows:

Step 1. Seated about two feet from the toilet.

Step 2. Seated about four feet from the toilet.

Step 3. Seated about six feet from the toilet.

Step 4. Seated out of direct view of the toilet.

Step 5. Free activities in any part of the activity area.

Step 6. Free activities in any part of the activity area, without the pants or toilet alarms. At this step you will need to check the learner's pants regularly.

Step 7. Free activities as in Step 6 and dressed in normal clothes.

Step 8. Free activities as in Step 7, but without extra drinks.

Physical Guidance

You may need to use physical guidance at Step 7 to teach the learner how to deal with trousers or skirts. Follow the learner into the toilet area and remain close in case this is necessary.

Pulling Trousers Down

Most handicapped persons, who can already pull their underpants down, usually cope with trousers by pulling them down with the underpants. You may need to use minimal guidance to direct his or her hands back to the underpants if they are left behind.

Dealing with Skirts

You may need to use guidance to teach the learner how to lift a skirt in order to get to the pants, and then again before sitting.

Pulling Trousers Up

If guidance is necessary, use it to establish the habit of pulling up the underpants first, then the trousers second.

Pulling Skirts Down

If guidance is necessary, use it to teach the learner to pull the skirt out of the pants all round.

When to Proceed to the Maintenance Phase

Once the learner has successfully toileted him or herself during normal activities, and while dressed in normal clothes, on at least eight out of ten voidings in a row, you can move on to the Maintenance Phase.

Maintenance Phase

Toileting Aim

The learner toilets him or herself, without prompts, guidance or accidents, in the normal environment for fourteen days in a row.

Environment

This part of the programme takes place all day everyday while the learner is awake. He or she should be involved in whatever activities and routines take place. No special routines or activities are necessary. The programme can be carried on at home, at school, and during outings and holidays. The aim is for the learner to transfer his or her new toileting skills to every situation. He or she should learn that everyone expects independent toileting. Consequently, it is those who live and work with the learner who carry out the Maintenance Phase. However, most learners transfer new skills better if they remain in the training environment for a few days or weeks so that the maintenance procedures are carried out there as well as at home. In this way, the range of activities and settings in which self-toileting occurs can be extended gradually. It also helps parents and direct-care staff become confident in using the new procedures.

Supervision of Maintenance

The trainer(s) who carried out Phases 1 to 7 should closely supervise this phase. This requires that:

1. You explain the procedures in detail to those who will use them. This includes the parents (if the learner lives at home), direct-care staff (if the learner lives in a residential centre), the teacher and teacher's aide (if the learner goes to school), and any other people who are regularly involved such as a physiotherapist, psychologist, speech therapist, etc.

2. Spend some time with any of these people demonstrating how to carry out the procedures if they have had no chance to be involved during training or if they appear to have difficulty understanding the procedures.

    This phase is crucial to the success of the programme, as the use of new toileting skills can be prevented by caregivers who either do everything for him or her or confuse, manipulate, or frighten the learner. Your guidance and confidence, the written records showing progress, and your reinforcement of them will help those using the procedures to try hard and to be consistent and thorough.

3. Regularly visit and/or phone those using the procedures to check on progress, solve problems, and renew the recording sheets. You need to be in contact about once a week. With some people you may need more frequent contact at first.

Procedure

Once the handicapped person has learned to look after his or her own toileting, there is still the need for some help until this new learning is fully established as a permanent part of life. There may be a few accidents until the learner is sure that everyone expects independent toileting. The learner must never be told to go to the toilet. Being directed to the toilet will cause the learner to wait for reminders and lose independence. However, if other persons are taken to the bathroom, the learner may go too, but should not be directed to the toilet in any way. The caregiver need not worry if the learner does not go to the toilet. The programme has taught him or her to hold on for long periods. The learner should have free access to the pot or toilet. If access is not freely available, he or she will have to rely on others or else have unavoidable accidents, returning to the old habits. The learner should always wear clothing that he or she can easily manage alone when toileting. Every pants check, toileting, and accident should be recorded on the record sheets provided (*see* Appendix C). This will tell the trainers and caregivers at a glance whether the learner is improving.

Pants Checks

Check whether the learner's pants are dry and clean before each meal, before morning and afternoon tea (or before leaving school), and before bed. The learner should also feel the pants. If he or she is dry and clean, give a big hug and praise. Do this with enthusiasm. It is a big achievement. Record these pants checks on the daily record sheet provided. No tangible reward is given during this phase.

Toileting

Watch the learner closely. If he or she goes towards the toilet or pot, follow without interfering. If voiding occurs in the toilet, wait until the pants are pulled up and then give enthusiastic praise. Record each toileting on the daily record sheet provided. The only time when it is permissible to direct the learner to the toilet is before an outing during which there may be no access to a toilet for several hours.

Accidents

If the learner is discovered wet or dirty, even if it is only a small patch, say "no" loudly and severely and point him or her to the toilet. Once the learner is seated, he or she should remain there for ten to fifteen minutes even if voiding occurs in the toilet. If he or she does not perform the toileting tasks correctly, use gentle guidance. If he or she does not remain seated, quietly use a touch or a point. Do not talk or look at the learner in any other way. Record all accidents on the daily record sheet provided. Do not praise toilet use after an accident. The number of accidents for each day should be recorded on a monthly sheet (*see* Appendix C). This will show at a glance whether the learner is improving.

Follow-Up

Your concern is that the learner has permanent use of the new toileting skills. Some handicapped persons in some environments forget some of the skills that they have learned. As with any other complex skill, some may need a second course of training to finally consolidate the skill. In addition, some parents, direct-care staff, or teachers may slip back into taking responsibility for their charge's toileting. Illness or hospitalisation or other family disruptions can sometimes cause the person to forget some of the toileting skills.

For all these reasons it is wise to contact those caring for the handicapped person, in order to assess his or her toileting skills, six months after the Maintenance Phase has been completed. This assessment should be similar to the assessment before the person was accepted into the programme.

Chapter 6

COMMON PROBLEMS
AND HOW TO HANDLE THEM

THIS PROGRAMME was tested by people whose normal work and lives were given to the care of handicapped persons. They included parents who sought toilet training for their own handicapped children, trained and student mental deficiency nurses and untrained staff working with handicapped people in a residential setting, and a number of volunteers who sought experience with handicapped persons. Most of them had considerable experience with handicapped persons. All of them were committed to helping the handicapped. Like you, they learned to use this programme by trying it. Unlike you, they did not have the information in this manual as a guide. This section describes many of the problems that they met and how they handled them.

Remember that handicapped persons who can benefit from this programme have already demonstrated considerable difficulty in learning not only toileting skills but also many other living skills. This programme is not a magic formula that miraculously causes these learning difficulties to disappear. It is because of these learning difficulties that such a detailed, step-by-step programme is necessary. Therefore, many of the problems described in this chapter will be familiar to anyone who has cared for and taught handicapped persons. Some of the problems are specific to the nature of bladder and bowel functioning.

When problems arise, they do not indicate failure on the part of either the learner or the trainer. Rather, they arise because of the handicaps of the learner, the complexity of bladder and bowel control, and the demands of the handicapped person's living environment.

Because each learner is a unique individual, you may well meet problems that have not been described here. The examples provided in this Chapter may inspire you to try your own solutions in such cases. Remember to rely on learning principles. These include careful recording of what you do and the results for the learner. This will enable you to pass on your successful solutions to others. It will also ensure that you do not continue with a solution that is ineffective and distressing for the learner.

Unsatisfactory Baseline Record

During the preliminary observation period, the aim is to get a stable record of toileting and voiding performance. This is the final chance to decide whether the individual handicapped person is likely to benefit from the programme.

Occasionally, during the first few days, toileting actually improves with no specific training. The number of accidents decreases or the person begins to go to the toilet alone and carry out all the toileting procedures perfectly. Mostly this occurs because the normal toileting pattern has been disrupted by the introduction of new people and a new situation. As these become familiar, the normal toileting pattern reappears.

We found that, in most cases, the improvement ceases after a few days. We continued the observation period until we had three days in a row during which there was no continuing improvement. This provided the true baseline. We were only able to see this changing pattern by graphing the toileting performance at the end of each day (*see* Appendices D and E).

Several children toileted themselves during baseline but still had accidents. Some toileted themselves occasionally but failed to carry out the full-toileting sequence correctly. They forgot to pull their pants up or down, sat incorrectly and voided on the floor, or carried out the tasks correctly without voiding. These children had learned some of the toileting tasks but had not joined them in the correct sequence. Some had not learned to recognize bladder or bowel signals.

These occurrences were not indications that the children were already capable of independent toileting, nor did they indicate that they were likely to learn without a structured programme. However, most of these children progressed rapidly during training.

In two cases, the improvement continued during the observation period until there was fully independent self-toileting with no accidents for three days in a row. Clearly, these children had the skills but were not using them in their normal environment. In these cases, the children immediately moved onto the Maintenance Phase of the programme. This was carried out by the usual caregivers under the supervision of the trainer. Each child became fully independent within a few weeks.

The Maintenance Phase used in this way helped the parents, teachers, and direct-care staff change their expectations to match the true ability of the child.

In one case this was quite difficult because the child continually repeated phrases in order to keep up a high level of interaction with adults. Asking to go to the toilet was one of these phrases. If he was ignored, he grew angry and often wet or soiled his pants. Part of the Maintenance Phase included ignoring his repeated toileting requests and any subsequent anger, while carrying out the normal maintenance procedures. In addition, his appropriate speech was encouraged whenever possible. This successfully reduced his toileting requests and established self-toileting without accidents as a normal part of his routine.

Difficult Behaviour During Training

Many handicapped persons who have experienced difficulty in learning complex skills have also developed a number of maladaptive behaviours, which actively interfere with learning. These behaviours have often enabled the person to avoid or escape the confusion, distress, or threat of failure that they have usually experienced when independence and skill is required of them.

A number of the children we worked with responded to direction with a wide range of resistive or maladaptive responses. These included running away, spitting, repetitive talking, refusing to move, self-induced vomiting, self-abusive behaviour such as hitting or biting, taking off clothes, shouting, throwing things, breaking or tearing objects, kicking, screaming, crying, stiffening, hitting, or pushing. Several children displayed some of these even when there was no direction being given. However, they mostly occurred when the child was being asked to sit still, pay attention, or finish a task, even though the activity may have been one that the child had chosen. These behaviours were not severe or frequent enough to exclude the children from training. However, the disruption to training that they caused required that they be dealt with.

Each instance of maladpative or resistive behaviour was met with gentle but firm insistence that the task be completed, while the difficult behaviour was completely ignored. A single instruction and physical guidance were used to ensure this when necessary. Completion of the task was followed by praise and affection, as well as a tangible reward if the task was a toileting task being taught at the time. In addition, appropriate play and interaction in between training sessions were also praised. This was sufficient in most cases to eliminate the difficult behaviour within a few days.

Some children with more severe behaviour difficulties did not respond to this treatment. These were children who threw full temper tantrums or hurt other children. This behaviour was eliminated by using systematic time-out from interaction. At the first occurrence of this behaviour, the trainer quickly and silently placed the child in a safe, empty room and closed the door. A kitchen timer was set to three minutes. If the child was quiet when the timer sounded, the trainer opened the door and gently brought the child back to the interrupted activity, at the same time giving praise and affection for the quiet behaviour. If the child was not quiet when the timer sounded, it was set for a further three minutes. On one occasion, a child remained in the room for twenty-one minutes. On several other occasions, another child was put back in the room several times one after the other. However, these instances only occurred during the first few days, followed rapidly by the complete elimination of the aggressive or tantrum behaviour.

These procedures were used to teach the child how to respond constructively rather than with extreme maladaptive responses. They were not intended to punish or to express the trainer's frustration or anger. For this reason, it was important that time-out was used systematically and that we recorded what we did and the frequency of the behaviour we were treating.

One child also exhibited violent tantrums and withheld voiding at the beginning of Phase 3 whenever she was seated on the toilet and prevented from getting off. The trainers decided that time-out in this situation would teach the child to use tantrums to avoid toileting. Consequently, they used guidance to keep the child seated. Two trainers relieved each other to ensure gentleness and reduce the stress on both the child and trainer. The tantrums gradually reduced in violence and length over three days. Once the child relaxed enough to void in the toilet, the tantrums stopped altogether and voiding began to occur immediately when the child was seated. Several other difficult behaviours were dealt with simply by a sharp, loud "no" just before they occurred. This was effective in eliminating self-induced vomiting and throwing of objects.

None of these behaviours could have been eliminated so effectively without also providing a great deal of pleasant interaction and activity as adaptive alternatives. This enabled the children to gain the attention and stimulation, which they sought originally through difficult behaviour, by more enjoyable and constructive means.

Behaviour of the Trainer

As the trainers learned to use this programme some of them found that their own behaviour occasionally created difficulties. This did not reflect any lack of care or commitment to the programme on their part. It did show how sensitive the children's learning processes were to the trainers' manner of presentation. The importance of personal style in education has been recognized for many years and it appears to be just as important when training handicapped persons in basic living skills.

Some trainers had such a hale and hearty style of movement and speaking that many of the children were overwhelmed by it and took very little initiative during trials. These trainers concentrated on speaking more gently and moving more slowly to give the children time to respond.

Other trainers were initially uncertain and timid when giving prompts, guidance, or rewards, so that the children appeared confused or took the opportunity to play around rather than concentrating on the task. Two or three trainers working together in the initial stages of the programme overcame this problem quickly.

Each trainer was able to gain support and confirmation from the others, as well as having a chance to discuss the procedures and observe others carrying them out.

Occasionally, a trainer made a mistake in prompting, guidance, or rewarding. This mainly occurred when a new procedure was beginning or when the trainer was acting quickly to keep up with the child's behaviour. Sometimes it was possible to relax for a few seconds, then start the trial again. At other times this was not possible. A note was made of that mistake on the record sheet, and that trial was not counted as part of the record of progress.

Problems During Phases 1 and 2

During these two phases there are no special procedures for toilet use or accidents, although these are recorded when they occur.

Voiding During Trials

Some children had a number of accidents during the half-hourly trials for pants up or standing. When this occurred, the trainer stopped the trial, cleaned up, and changed the child's pants. If the child began to void but then stopped the stream, he was seated on the toilet. The trainer waited for a few minutes or until voiding occurred in the toilet and then cleaned up and put clean pants on the child. The trainer and child then went back to the toilet and the trials were continued. These accidents may have sometimes been a behaviour the child used to avoid carrying out the trials. However, they were more likely to indicate that going into the toilet and having the pants pulled down had already become a signal to relax the perineal muscles.

This may have also been the case when a child frequently voided in the toilet when he had been seated ready for the prompt to stand from the toilet. When this happened, the trainer waited for voiding to finish and then continued with the trials.

Noncompliance During Trials

Some children demonstrated during baseline observations that they could stand up and pull their pants up, and yet needed considerable guidance during trials. These children tried to sit, pulled their pants down, grizzled, waved their hands about, or made no move at all. Some trainers felt that this occurred either because they were not carrying out the procedures correctly or because the child was unable to learn. This was rarely the case, although all trainers found that the physical guidance technique took some time to perfect. Usually, the child had not learned to attend or respond to direction. It was this skill, rather than the first two toileting skills, that had to be learned.

During the first few days, trainers had to use a great deal of guidance to correctly position the child and get his or her attention before giving the prompt. In these cases progress was slow during the first two phases. However, most children learned to attend and respond well enough during these phases so that progress through later phases was more rapid.

Problems During Mealtimes

Ideally, training should continue throughout the day, including during mealtimes. Staff arrangements should allow for this. We did not find this difficult during Phases 1 and 2 or during Steps 5 to 8 of Phase 7. However, it did cause problems during the other parts of the programme. Lunch was eaten in a dining area of the unit in which the toilets were situated. This meant that the children were not sitting in front of the toilets during mealtimes. When the pants alarm sounded during lunch, the trainer carried out the appropriate procedures. The only variation was that the child had to go further to reach the toilet. Once the toileting procedure was finished, the child returned to the meal table.

If you decide that training should be discontinued during lunchtime, make the nontraining time as short as possible. There are several problems that may arise as a result of the lunch break and that will have to be planned for. Training may take longer than our estimates indicate. There may be a consistently high rate of accidents during the lunch break that do not reduce either in size or frequency. Several procedures may help overcome this problem. Carry out a pants check, as used in the Maintenance Phase described in Chapter 6, before the learner sits at the table and as each course of the meal is presented. This may increase the learner's ability to hold back voiding until the meal has finished.

In the event of an accident at the table, unclip the pants alarm, say "no" loudly, and remove the food for a fixed period of time, for example, three minutes. Do not change the learner's pants until training begins again. At the recommencement of training, place the learner's hand on the wet or soiled pants and carry out the appropriate toileting procedure as if the accident had just occurred. If the accident is so messy that you cannot leave the learner in the wet or soiled pants, say "no" loudly, remove the learner from the table, and clean up and change the pants without speaking and with as little contact with the learner as possible. Under these circumstances it may be effective to withdraw the rest of the meal completely. An occasional missed meal should do no harm. However, you will need to keep a record of how often this occurs to ensure that your procedures are effective.

Difficulty with Prompts

Some children began to carry out the required toileting task before the trainer had time to give the prompt. This occurred during Phases 1, 2, 4, and 5. It was more of a problem when the child had just had an accident and was in a hurry to get onto the toilet. Other children would not look towards the trainer so that the prompt could be given.

Trainers were careful to prevent the child from moving, so that he was quiet and still when the prompt was given. It was important that all children waited for the prompt unless it had been completely faded out. Progressing through each sequence of steps and prompts ensured that the child had a similar level of confidence and automatic performance for each skill. In this way, performance of the whole toileting sequence later in the programme was more likely to be smooth, with no uncertainty or forgetting. In addition, requiring that children wait for the prompt during Phases 4 and 5 helped many of them develop better bowel and bladder control.

Problems with Drinking

Some children refused drinks, and it was clear that they were resisting direction rather than not wanting to drink. The use of force or scolding to make them drink only distressed the children or caused them to resist drinking even more. One or two children only accepted drinks after several days of reward for taking a mouthful at a time. They were rewarded for drinking with the next page of a story book, a song, or some other activity that they were wanting at the time. Other children drank sufficient when it was offered a quarter or half a cup at a time. Some drank more when they were offered two or three different beverages to choose from. If a child handed back an unfinished drink, the trainer gently motioned him to finish it. However, if the child still did not drink, there was no pressure to make him.

On rare occasions a drink was tipped out or dribbled. Children who did this were supervised closely and given careful guidance to ensure that they always held the cup correctly and drank carefully. A towel was placed on the child's lap to protect his pants. No child was denied drinks when he spilled or dribbled, as the extra fluids were a necessary part of training. A spilled drink was always replaced and the child prompted to finish it. Some trainers shouted a loud "no" when spilling was deliberate and then gave guidance if necessary.

Unusual Accidents

Once the learner was wearing a pants alarm and sitting in the toilet area, most accidents occurred on the chair. However, all voidings that came to rest outside the toilet bowl were defined as accidents. This included voiding on the floor while walking to the toilet, and voiding on the toilet seat, pants, or floor while being seated, standing from the toilet, or actually sitting on the toilet. All of these were dealt with as accidents, even if the child was in the process of toileting and even if all other toileting tasks were performed correctly. The trainer said a loud, sharp "no" and recorded the accident on the record sheet.

Accidents on the Way to the Toilet

As training progressed, some children got up to go to the toilet by themselves, but began voiding on the way. This indicated that they were learning the signs of bladder or bowel tension, but were not yet responding quickly enough or holding back voiding for long enough. Frequently, the accident was no more than a damp patch on the pants. The trainers dealt with this as with any accident, i.e. by saying "no" and carrying out the toileting procedure for that phase. The children were not allowed to carry through their self-initiation. No toileting that was accompanied by any form of accident was recorded as a self-initiation.

Sometimes these accidents did not touch the studs in the pants, and the accident was not noticed until the child was already on the toilet. Trainers learned to observe the pants very carefully to check for this. They said "no," while putting the child's hand on the wet pants, and recorded and treated it as an accident.

This was particularly a problem for two children, who frequently voided a tiny drop into their pants. If the pants were left on, these drops eventually accumulated until there was enough moisture to set off the pants alarm. One child had a long history of this behaviour, commonly known as "dribble incontinence." He had had surgery several years earlier, which was successful, but continued to void small drops during the day. The problem was overcome by trainers observing his pants closely and carrying out the accident and toileting procedure every time a small drop appeared on the pants, whether or not the pants alarm sounded. This child became fully independent in toileting, and his dribbling did not occur again.

Accidents While Seated on the Toilet

A number of children voided on the seat or floor while seated on the toilet. Careful observation showed that some of these children were not seating themselves correctly or were moving out of the correct position after being seated. This indicated that guidance for sitting or remaining seated during Phases 3 or 4 had not been careful enough.

The correct sitting position should be with the torso upright or leaning forward. The trainer used guidance to prevent children from leaning back or wriggling forward onto the edge of the seat. However, even with this guidance, some boys still voided out of the toilet. In these cases, the penis tended to point up naturally or lift up whenever urination began. Mostly, careful guidance to lean forward and sit with legs parted successfully overcame this problem. A few boys learned to hold the penis down by hand, but not many children were skilled enough to cope with such fine adjustments of behaviour. Several boys could only overcome this problem on a full-sized toilet. They could not achieve the careful adjustment of posture required on a small toilet or pot.

Accidents While Getting Off the Toilet

Several children voided in the toilet, stood and pulled their pants up, but the pants alarm sounded within the next few seconds. In several cases this was because urine had collected on pubic hair or at the the end of the penis. These instances were *not* treated as accidents. In normal life they would not be a problem. However, they were a problem while pants alarms were being used. The trainers solved this problem in several ways. Some children were wiped just before they pulled their pants up. One or two began to wipe themselves. If wiping disrupted the child's performance, the trainer waited until the child was back on his chair and then changed his pants.

Several children wet their pants, the toilet seat, or the floor as they were standing. They were not remaining seated long enough to finish voiding. The use of careful guidance to ensure that they remained seated until voiding was finished solved this problem.

Unusual Voiding Patterns

Two children voided much more frequently than usual during the baseline observations and training. One child toileted himself as often as every fifteen to thirty minutes, but often began voiding in his pants on the way to the toilet. This was the usual pattern, and there was no evidence of physical abnormality or infection.

This child quickly reached Phase 7, but the extra fluids increased toileting to every few minutes. Observation showed that this child was only voiding small amounts in the toilet each time. The programme was altered so that the child had to remain on the toilet for twenty minutes each time toileting occurred. Initially, a great deal of guidance was required to keep him sitting quietly. During each twenty-minute toileting he voided a small amount up to nine or ten times. The number of voidings during each toileting and the time between getting up from the toilet and the next toileting were recorded on the back of the record sheet. The number of voidings during toileting decreased over a few days to two or three. Originally, it was intended that this procedure would continue until there were at least seven toiletings in a row with twenty minutes in between. However, the times initially increased a little, but over two more days there was no further increase. The trainers reverted to the usual procedures and accepted that they could not expect a drop in frequency of voiding. However, once the extra drinks were stopped during Phase 7, the child began to void only five or six times a day and maintained this frequency during and after the Maintenance Phase.

Several other children only voided small amounts in the toilet. They appeared unable to completely relax the perineum or tightened it again immediately when voiding began. In a few cases, this problem disappeared within the first few days on Phase 3. If the problem remained, extra reward was offered for completing voiding. The trainer held the reward within the child's sight and presented it with praise as soon as more urine was voided. This successfully overcame the problem within a day or two.

Learning Disrupted by Previously Learned Behaviour

Some children came to us with a long history of inappropriate toileting behaviour that had to be unlearned before the new toileting tasks could be learned.

Staying on the Toilet for Long Periods

Several children had developed the habit of sitting on the toilet for long periods, whether they had voided or not. These were generally children who were profoundly or severely retarded and showed little interest in their environment.

Trainers found that these children took a long time to learn to stand from the toilet during Phase 2. Once prompting had stopped, they waited for a hand movement or a soft touch before they would stand. Trainers put much more careful effort into fading out the guidance, and all the children were eventually able to move onto Phase 3. However, they often reverted later in the programme to remaining seated after voiding in the toilet, and guidance was again necessary.

Kicking Off Pants While on the Toilet

A few children had developed the habit of taking their pants right off on the way to the toilet or kicking them off after they were seated. Trainers stayed close to these children during toileting so that they could immediately use guidance to prevent this. Extra care with guidance was needed to teach these children to keep their hands and legs still while sitting on the toilet. This careful use of guidance was usually successful in eliminating this problem.

Standing Instead of Sitting to Void

Some boys had learned to stand to void in the toilet. Trainers allowed this the first few times. However, if the children were having any bowel accidents or were at any time inaccurate when aiming the stream into the toilet, standing during toileting was prevented by using guidance. The trainer kept his or her hands close during toileting so that guidance could be used to turn the child around to sit. If the child self-initiated toileting, the trainer followed the child ready to give guidance in the same way. Self-initiations that required guidance were recorded, with a note indicating that guidance to sit was needed. No self-initiations requiring this guidance were counted as full self-initiations. The child had to self-initiate ten times in a row without guidance before he could move onto Phase 7.

One child habitually had bowel accidents. As soon as this happened, he went into the toilet, pulled his pants down, leaned over with his hands on the seat, and presented his buttocks to be wiped. Although he learned to void urine in the toilet, he still carried out this procedure for every bowel motion. The trainers eliminated this behaviour by using two procedures in addition to the normal training procedures. Everytime the child went into the toilet, whether it was following a bladder or bowel accident or to self-initiate, the trainer was ready to use guidance to prevent him from leaning over the toilet. If, during a self-initiation, this interfered so that the child stopped pulling his pants down or just stood still, he was directed back to his chair. In addition, the child was guided to stand up straight, facing away from the toilet whenever he needed to be wiped after a bowel movement. After a few days the problem never occurred again.

Asking to Go to the Toilet

A number of children had learned to ask every time they wanted to go to the toilet. All toileting requests were ignored during training. This sometimes took a great deal of self-control because the children were either very appealing or insistent. It was also very clear at times that the children were dying to go to the toilet. However, it was important to let them have accidents if they did not self-initiate. The accident procedure was a very important part of the teaching technique.

Problems During Phases 4 and 5

The important learning tasks during these two phases were to stop voiding when it began away from the toilet and hold the sphincter closed for increasingly longer periods, so that the learner had time to pull down the pants and sit on the toilet before relaxing the perineum. While these tasks were being learned, a few problems occasionally arose.

Inability to Stop the Urine Flow Following Accidents

Most children continued urinating on some occasions while they were being taken to the toilet. Others could stop the flow, but began urinating during prompting or guidance for pants down and sitting. Trainers concentrated on saying "no" loudly enough so that it was startling. After a number of trials, this usually induced the children to stop the flow. This improvement could be seen in the daily record of the level of accident, which gradually decreased. If the flow started again before the child was seated, the trainer again said "no" loudly. This was usually effective over a few days or weeks. Occasionally a child showed no signs of learning these skills and, despite our procedures, was only partially independent in toileting by the end of the programme. Mostly these were the children who were neurologically damaged. They were cerebrally palsied or epileptic and may not have had the nervous pathways to allow bladder control. However, this was only an assumption on our part. There may be other procedures that we did not try that may have induced the learning of bladder control by these children.

Difficulty with Sitting and Pants Down

A few children were unable to get themselves on to the toilet. These were small children who did not put the usual effort into hoisting themselves onto the seat. The toilet was not too large, as other children of their size managed with no trouble. Initially, they needed very careful and detailed guidance. The hands were guided to hold onto the wall and the side of the seat, while one leg was guided up to enable the buttock to lodge on the edge of the seat. Then the child's hands were guided behind him to the edge of the seat, and the hips were gently pushed so that the child wriggled back into the correct sitting position.

Other children were able to sit but did not respond to the prompt or were so distracted by the accident that they could not concentrate on this task. Some children also had difficulty learning to pull their pants down for the same reasons. For all these children the toileting trials were not frequent enough to enable them to steadily progress. The trainers introduced three trials for sitting or pants down every half hour in the same format as during Phases 1 and 2. These trials were recorded on the back of the daily record sheet in the same way as for Phases 1 and 2.

When three trials in a row without guidance were achieved at a prompt during the half-hourly trials, trainers waited for three successful toiletings without guidance for that skill before moving onto the next prompt. This continued through the prompts until the toileting aim for that·Phase was achieved.

It was important that the pants were always pulled down to knee level. This not only prevented them from slipping off while the child was on the toilet, but also ensured that they were clear of the toilet when the child sat. Many children needed guidance to achieve this. If this was not taught carefully, many children began to pull their pants down only partway later in the programme. Consequently, the pants were often wet while the child was voiding in the toilet, and progress was disrupted.

Illness During Training

Several children had bouts of diarrhoea during training. If a bowel motion in the pants was clearly too loose to be controlled, it was recorded as an accident, but a note was made to indicate that it was unavoidable. Usually, dietary control was successful in reducing this problem within a day or two. Occasionally, the child had other symptoms of bacterial infection, and the medical practioner prescribed medication.

One child had constantly loose bowels, which would normally have excluded her from training. However, Metamucil® was given each morning for a few days before training and the problem disappeared. Metamucil was continued during training and maintenance, and the child became fully independent in toileting. In this particular instance, the family diet was probably at fault. However, the family was unwilling to make any dietary alterations. The child completed training and maintenance, but follow-up six months later showed that this family has stopped using Metamucil, and the child had reverted to having frequent diarrhoea. In addition, she had begun to have bladder accidents, although she still occasionally toileted herself. This child should not have been accepted into the programme without clear evidence of normal bowel functioning for at least six months.

If a child became ill enough to be distressed, training was stopped until the child had recovered. This only occurred with two children, who were absent from training for only one day. Generally, minor ailments were treated or left to take their course while training continued. Trainers took the normal precautions to ensure that the child was warm and comfortable.

One child had several grand mal seizures during training. The treatment normally used for that child was followed and training stopped for several hours following a seizure while the child slept.

Performing Toileting Tasks Inappropriately

Some children began to pull their pants down out in the activity area or at home during the training period. This also occurred occasionally while the child was in the toilet area. These children were clearly practising their new skills, as children often do when they are learning a new behaviour. Some children continued to do this during the Maintenance Phase. During training the trainers used a point and minimal guidance if necessary to ensure that the pants were left alone, while giving as little attention to the child as possible. At the same time, other more appropriate activities were rewarded with attention from the trainers. If the behaviour still occurred during the Maintenance Phase, caregivers were instructed to do the same. Usually, this behaviour disappeared quickly.

Problems During Phase 7

During Phase 7, children had to cope with an increasing number of distractions as they moved further from the toilet. They also had to put more effort into holding back voiding and going to the toilet. This created problems for some children.

Repeated Accidents

A few children began to have accidents again when they were moved further away from the toilet or were free to play in the activity area. If a child had three accidents in a row during any of the steps in Phase 7, they were taken back to sit two feet from the toilet. The trainer then proceeded through the steps again. Mostly this was all that was required to again establish accident-free self-toileting. Occasionally, this was not effective. In these cases, the trainers added two new procedures to the programme. The steps in moving the child further from the toilet were made smaller. This was usually only necessary once the toilet was out of the child's view. Small steps included free activity in the bathroom area with the toilet in sight, then in the bathroom area and a small area outside the bathroom, then in half the room just off the bathroom, and so on. In addition, the trainers required a greater number of perfect self-toiletings in a row before moving on to the next step.

Inappropriate Behaviour During Toileting

Some children began playing around while they were taking themselves to the toilet. This occurred as the trainers' close control of their toileting gradually reduced. This was less likely to happen if, during earlier training phases, the trainers had gradually removed themselves further from the child while he or she was toileting. This allowed the toilet and the child's own behavioural cues to control toileting behaviour rather than the close presence of the trainer. However, while becoming more removed from the toilet area, the trainers had to remain alert and be ready to move in and give guidance the instant the child began to behave inappropriately.

If, despite this process, the child still played around during self-toileting, guidance was used and that trial was not counted as a self-initiation. Playing around was especially a problem if it led to an accident, as this meant that the number of rewards were reduced. When this occurred, the child often became upset. Usually guidance quickly overcame this problem. However, it may have sometimes been more effective to reintroduce the phase which teaches that skill which is being disrupted by the inappropriate play. If you do this, you may need to allow self-initiation, but follow the child and use the prompts as required for that phase. With this procedure you may also need to wait for a greater number of performances in a row without guidance before moving onto the next prompt or phase.

Self-Initiated Toileting Without Voiding

Occasionally a child was so keen to be rewarded that he or she went to the toilet without voiding. These performances were ignored, no reward was given, and the child was directed back to the chair or play. This effectively eliminated this problem.

Problems of Bowel Control

Occasionally a child became fully independent for bladder voiding, but not for bowel movements. Although bowel control is usually learned before bladder control by most children, this does not appear to be the case for some handicapped children. It may be that bladder control is learned more quickly by these children because of the greater frequency of bladder voiding. This greater frequency gives more opportunity to practise toileting skills and to link these skills to the cues of bladder tension. Bowel movements are about a day apart, on the average, and this longer time gives the child more chance to forget the sensation of bowel tension. In addition, bowel movements are more difficult to hold back than bladder voiding. Consequently, some children who usually went to the toilet to have bowel movements frequently began to void just before they reached the toilet.

If this was a problem during training, it usually continued for some time during the Maintenance Phase. Occasionally the problem only arose once the Maintenance Phase began. Usually, bowel control was eventually achieved during the Maintenance Phase as long as the procedures were kept to consistently. However, in these cases this phase took longer than it did for children who had no problems with bowel control. However, some children did not achieve bowel control. A separate training programme especially for bowel control is necessary in these cases (Bettison, 1979).

Failure to Reach Criterion

The measure of success during training is fully independent self-toileting over several days with no more than two accidents during that time. A small number of children did not reach this criterion while we were testing the programme. Because the programme was being tested, a time limit of seven weeks was placed on the length of training. Most children who did not reach criterion probably would have if we had continued training for longer than seven weeks.

Several children remained at Phases 4, 5, or 6 for several weeks, with only slow progress. In all cases these were children who sought adult guidance or approval before they carried out many of their everyday activities. Two of them also failed to reduce the level of accidents. Although these children may have eventually reached criterion with a longer period of training, the cost, in terms of trainer time and morale and frustration or boredom for the learner, may not justify an extended period of training. These children may make acceptable improvement if a different training programme is used that concentrates on only a few of the toileting skills. They may be able to learn to pull their pants up and down, seat themselves appropriately on the toilet, extend the time between voidings, toilet themselves in response to a prompt, or indicate when they need to go to the toilet.

Problems During the Maintenance Phase

A number of problems arose during this phase. Although it was crucial that the usual caregivers carried out the procedures, they were not always consistent or confident. Sometimes the nature of the procedures conflicted with their usual methods of handling the child. Sometimes illness or other events interrupted the programme so that the procedures could not be carried out. Staff changes in the residential setting also frequently disrupted the programme. Occasionally, other less significant people in the child's environment consistently interfered with the procedure or undermined the usual caregivers' commitment.

The trainers had very little control over the child's environment and had to rely heavily on human relations skills and careful, specific information giving. Many problems were minor, and each one required different handling. Generally, they were solved by applying basic learning principles: defining the problem, devising a clearly defined method, ensuring that the method was possible in that environment, and providing the caregivers with feedback and encouragement.

Anticipated Problems of Skill Transfer to the Normal Environment

Some handicapped persons may live in environments that you consider will actively interfere with the transfer of their newly learned toileting skills.

Others may recognize and respond appropriately to bladder and bowel tension in the structured environment provided by this programme, but have difficulty in the relatively unstructured environment in which they live. Our experience with other training programmes suggests that these two problems are more likely to be overcome if the person remains in the training environment for some time after the completion of training. The maintenance programme should be carried out during this period, together with a range of structured and free activities. This will allow the handicapped person to consolidate the new skills and provide an opportunity for more systematic teaching of the maintenance procedures to caregivers and others involved with the person. It would also allow the trainers to gradually introduce an increasing number of situations that are likely to interfere with toileting performance in the person's usual environment. This consolidation period may be especially beneficial for persons who live in institutions where there are frequent changes in direct-care staff.

The optimum length of time for consolidation would depend on the progress of the individual learner both during training and during the consolidation period itself. It should also take into account the difficulties in the person's usual environment. For example, a person whose family includes two children under four years and a new baby may benefit from a longer consolidation period than a person who lives with adults only.

When a consolidation period is necessary, the trainers, caregivers, and the handicapped person whenever possible should together agree on a performance target that is to be met before the Maintenance Phase is transferred to the natural environment. Progress should be reviewed at the end of each week to enable adjustments to the programme or the performance target when necessary.

Frequent Accidents During Maintenance

It is not unusual for the number of accidents to increase during the first few days or weeks of maintenance. Usually they quickly decrease again. The trainer warned caregivers that this was likely. This pattern is common when the social and physical environment in which recently learned behaviour occurs is changed.

However, a few children continued to have more than one accident every two or three days. Sometimes this was just one aspect of a common pattern of difficult behaviour from the child and inappropriate responses from the adult. This maladaptive pattern between parent and child was markedly reduced during training in most cases, because the parents took part in the training. They developed more positive expectations and new methods of child management. However, some playing around during toileting or purposeful accidents still occurred in the home environment away from the training unit. Moreover, teachers and other family members could not be part of the training. The problem during the Maintenance Phase often occurred only in relation to one of these people. Several children appeared unable to maintain their independence without the highly structured routines of the training unit. These children were often more independent in the structured school programme than at home.

Occasionally, careful questioning or observation of the caregivers showed that they were not carrying out the procedures correctly, although general child management was effective. In most cases, these problems were corrected after the trainer spent more time demonstrating the procedures and prompting the caregivers while they carried them out. More frequent visits and phone calls and positive feedback about their performance and the child's progress also led to improvement. However, one child had to be transferred to a different school so that this phase could be carried out during school time.

In one case the accidents did not decrease, despite excellent performance on the part of the child's parents. The prompts for toileting were reintroduced. They were given at the normal voiding times and were faded out again in the same way as during Phase 6. This child was having few accidents by the end of the Maintenance Phase and only needed occasional toileting prompts. Another child stopped having accidents, after the introduction of a point and a nod from the caregiver, whenever the child asked to go to the toilet.

Failure to Self-Initiate Toileting

It is important to remember that the aim of this programme is to give the learner full independence in toileting. This independence is crucial in building the person's own self-confidence as well as other's positive acceptance of him or her as an independent person with the potential to learn and develop. Consequently, any decision to provide direction in toileting after training should be a last resort after all other attempts to maintain independence have failed.

If you decide that the learner requires toileting reminders or prompts to remain accident-free during or after the Maintenance Phase, these should be systematically faded to as little as possible. There are two aspects that should be faded. The prompts can be faded to become less intrusive by using the same fading method as is used during training. This may allow parents and others to eventually use no more than an unobtrusive gesture when they wish to remind the handicapped person to go to the toilet. In this way, neither need feel embarrassed or unusual, especially in social situations.

The other aspect that should be faded is the frequency of toileting prompts. While the learner may not be able to altogether manage without prompts, they can be reduced considerably by tying them to regular activities such as after getting out of bed, before going to the table for meals, before going out to play, before going on outings or going to bed, and after arriving home from school. Gradually, toileting should become an habitual part of at least some of these activities so that the handicapped person automatically goes to the toilet without a reminder. Moreover, it provides caregivers with a structure that reduces the common anxiety about toileting and the common tendency to give more toileting directions than are required.

Problems for Caregivers

Some parents found it difficult to relax their supervision and direction of the child during this phase. They were unwilling to allow him or her to have accidents and grew anxious when voiding had not occurred for an hour or two. This sometimes resulted in the child looking for direction for toileting and an increase in accidents. Most parents relaxed more once it was pointed out that the procedure that followed accidents was an important learning experience for the child. The trainer also explained that the child was likely to make mistakes while learning to attach the new skills to each situation in which bladder or bowel tension occurred. The parents' attention was always directed to the competence of their child shown in all the self-initiated toiletings that they had recorded.

Most problems or concerns that the caregivers expressed were easily reduced by clear information about their child's performance, the nature of learning, the experiences of other trainers and caregivers, and the effects of expectations on learners.

Failure to Improve

Most children reached the maintenance criterion of fourteen days of accident-free self-toileting in a row within a few weeks; an occasional child took several months. We did not continue this phase longer than six months. Children who had continued that long were usually showing no further signs of improvement. In addition, the caregivers by then were habitually using the procedures as part of their normal child management. Two children had not reached criterion by the end of six months but continued to improve after this phase was withdrawn. The few children who had not reached the training criterion, but had learned a number of new toileting skills, were put on a modified maintenance programme designed to maintain those skills. The programme was tailored to suit each individual child and environment.

In one case the Maintenance Phase was stopped after eight weeks. The accident rate was increasing, and the child was rarely performing any of the toileting tasks independently. More intensive procedures would probably have helped, but the caregivers felt unable to give anymore time in a situation where one person was often in sole charge of eight to ten children. This child's toileting and general behaviour will be reviewed every six months until there is some indication that another attempt at toilet training is warranted.

Problems After Maintenance

Usually, systematic programmes that are firmly based on careful assessment and task analysis are successful in teaching skills, and this programme is no exception. However, we occasionally found that a person stopped using the skill sometime after the Maintenance Phase had been completed. If you meet this problem, it will not necessarily reflect on you or the programme. The establishment of new skills as an habitual part of a person's life requires not only training and procedures to transfer the new learning, but also continued practice and an environment that encourages those skills. Most of us have had the experience of learning a complex skill and finding that we have had to relearn at least some part of the skill after a change of life-style or a period of no practice. The same problem can occur with toileting. We have retrained several children who were independent in toileting earlier but who were no longer reliably toileting themselves after being institutionalised or after a series of rapid staff changes that resulted in widely varying care and a loss of skill.

As trainers we need to be aware of the problems of environmental and organizational management that may prevent independence. Sometimes the successful acquisition of skills by handicapped persons depends more on these factors than on training. The intervention required to alter these factors may also take more time and effort than the provision of training.

The purpose of this manual is not to provide guidelines for major re-organizations of this nature. They may involve family intervention, community action, organizational restructuring, political action, or legislation. However, teaching new toileting skills to persons who are prevented from using them may cause considerable frustration and loss of independence and motivation. Consequently, we hope that those who are concerned to provide training for handicapped persons will also extend their interests and skills to these larger areas of change.

APPENDICES

Appendix A
DESCRIPTION OF ALARMS
AND HOW TO SERVICE THEM

DESCRIPTION OF ALARMS AND HOW TO SERVICE THEM

Urine Alarm*

Urine alarms are electronically simple devices (Azrin, Bugle, and O'Brien, 1971; Van Wagenen and Murdock, 1966) that make toilet training quicker (Azrin and Foxx, 1971; Madsen et al., 1969; Mahoney, Van Wagenen, and Meyerson, 1971; Van Wagenen et al., 1969). Unfortunately, construction details for these designs are not usually published so that they can be built only by the electronically sophisticated.

A recent article (Zimmer-Hart, 1977) that contained some construction details appeared more successful in helping parents and other caregivers to build a urine alarm. This appendix extends that article by providing both a printed-circuit-board pattern and an illustration of the finished alarm.

What an Alarm Does

A urine alarm detects the presence of urine by using a safe, small electric current. The detector current is amplified to operate a light, a buzzer, or some other alarm. The device consumes very little power when urine is absent so that it can be battery powered.

The alarm described here uses a single CMOS integrated circuit to detect the presence of urine. A transistor amplifier then operates a buzzer (*see* Fig. 1).

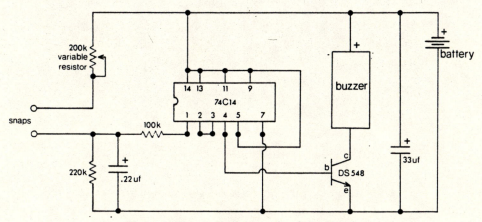

Figure 1. Electronic Schematic of the Circuit

How the Alarm Works

Urine, which contains body salts, conducts eletricity. When urine is present between the two snaps, current flows from the "+" (positive) side of the battery to point A in the circuit. The maximum current is only 30/1,000,000 ampere, which is very safe. The current then flows on to point B, where any electrical interference is removed by the .22 uf capacitor.

The current is detected by the 74C14 integrated circuit, which then supplies current to the DS 548 transitor, turning it on. This operates the buzzer.

The sensitivity is set by adjusting the 200K variable resistor. The sensitivity must be adjusted to keep the alarm turned off when no urine is present.

*Charles L. Hart, Department of Psychology, Flinders University, developed the alarm and provided the description of its construction. Support for the alarm design was provided by Flinders University (Project 267) and by Orana Inc., Parkside, South Adelaide 5061, Australia.

Printed Circuit Board Design

The actual printed circuit board for the alarm is shown in Figure 2. An illustration of the completed alarm is shown in Figure 3.

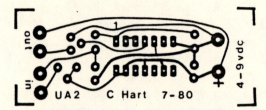

Figure 2. The Printed Circuit Board Pattern

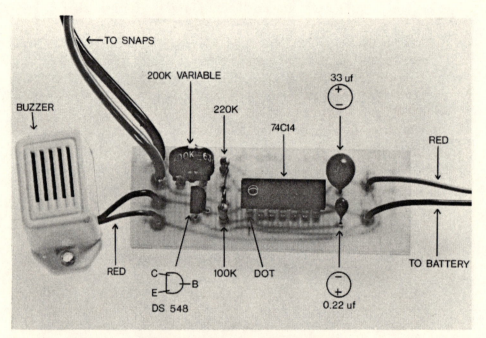

Figure 3. A Completed Circuit Board

To make an alarm, first buy all the parts shown in Table I. Next have the printed circuit board made from a negative of Figure 2. Drill all holes with a No. 60 (1 mm) bit.

Using a fine tip, 270°-300° centigrade soldering iron, install all parts shown in Figure 3 except the 74C14 and the battery. Note that most parts must be installed in a particular orientation; check the location of the "+," "dot," and "c, b, e." When connecting the wire do not cut it to length until you have determined how much is needed as shown in this chapter in a section on connecting the snaps to the pants and toilet alarms. After checking that all these parts are correctly installed, solder-in the 74C14. When this is in place and checked, connect the battery.

Table I. Parts List*

1 Printed Circuit Board Marked "UA2"

RESISTORS

1 100K, 1/4-watt resistor (brown-black-yellow)
1 220K, 1/4-watt resistor (red-red-yellow)
1 200K minature variable resistor
1 5K6, 1/4-watt resistor (green-blue-red)

CAPACITORS

1 .22 uf, tantalum capacitor
1 33 uf, tantalum capacitor

SOLID-STATE DEVICES

1 DS 548 transistor
1 74C14 hex Schmidt trigger

BATTERY

1 9-volt transistor battery
1 battery lead

BUZZER

1 9-volt transistor buzzer

CASE

1 plastic case
2 rubber grommets
1 metre flexible wire

ATTACHMENTS

1 packet of snaps (Gripper brand, junior size are suitable)
2 small stainless steel screws and nuts
   epoxy resin (Araldite is suitable)

---

*Most electronic parts listed here are available at any electronics chain store

Set the Sensitivity

The alarm should sound only when current is passing through urine. If the alarm is too sensitive, water or sweat will set it off. On the other hand, if it is too insensitive, it will miss some accidents.

Before trying to set the sensitivity, first check that the alarm is working when maximum current flows. Touch the two snaps together. If the alarm does not sound, find the variable resistor on the PCB and adjust it while touching the snaps together. If the alarm still does not sound, disconnect the battery and check the wiring. If the wiring is correct, some part is defective. If the alarm sounds, all parts are in order.

Get the 5K6 resistor you did not use in construction. Hold the snaps so that they touch the wire leads of the resistor, but so that your fingers do not make contact with the snaps. Next, find the variable resistor on the PCB and move it to the end of its range in which the alarm is silent. Now slowly move it back in the opposite direction until the buzzer just begins to "chirp." The sensitivity is now adjusted for 5,600 Ohms (5K6) resistance.

A a check, remove the 5K6 resistor and hold one of the snaps in each hand. The alarm should not sound.

Maintenance

The battery should last about a year in average use. Remove it when the alarm is not used for more than a week. The alarm is not waterproof and will be damaged if left in water. If accidently wetted, quickly remove the battery, shake off any water you can see, and allow the alarm to dry completely before reconnecting the battery.

Some sensitivity adjustment may be required for clients with very dilute urine (more sensitivity) or very heavy sweating (less sensitivity).

Putting the Alarm in a Case

The alarm case should be as small as possible. We used a small plastic box with a metal cover that is screwed on (*see* Fig. 4).

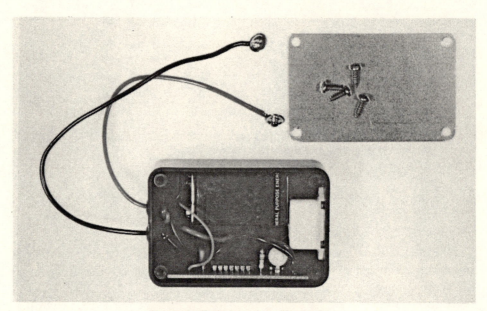

Figure 4. The Alarm in a Plastic Case

Drill two holes in the side of the case and install grommets for the two wires going to the snaps. Snaps made for clothes can be used by soldering the wires to the edges of the snaps.

The case can be supported with a fabric belt or held against clothes with Velcro®. For a smaller child a belt is preferable, because the weight of the alarm may pull the pants down.

The Pants and Toilet Alarms

The pants and toilet alarms can be constructed by anyone with the following instructions. Several members of our training team have constructed and repaired similar alarms without any previous experience. Intellectually handicapped persons have also been successful with a small amount of training. No electronic knowledge is required.

Soldering

If you have never used a soldering iron, it would be useful to practice with scrap wire a few times before constructing the alarms. The soldering iron should be at full temperature. Allow it to heat for several minutes after switching it on. When it is hot, touch the tip of the iron to the solder until it has collected a small bubble of solder. You can allow the iron to cool with the solder on it if you need time to place the end of the wire to be soldered into position on the part to be connected. Reheat the iron and touch the hot tip containing the bubble of solder over this connection until the joint is completely covered by solder. Ensure that the entire connection is filled with solder so that there are no air bubbles. The wire should be firmly lodged in the solder so that it does not move when you push it gently.

The Training Pants

The urine alarm used to detect voiding accidents is attached to ordinary underpants that the trainee wears during training. The pants should be a comfortable fit, but loose enough so that the trainee can easily insert his/her hands at the waist and so that they slide up and down easily over the hips. At least eight pairs of underpants should be provided for each trainee. If washing and drying facilities are not readily available during training, more underpants may be needed. The underpants contain moisture-detecting snaps to which the flexible wires from the alarm are connected.

Connecting the Snaps to the Pants

The indented halves of two snaps are hammered on to the pants. They are placed in a position where they are most likely to be dampened at the beginning of the urine flow. This position varies between individuals. Generally, the snaps should be placed for men and boys about 1.3 centimetres below where the tip of the penis touches the underpants. For women and girls, the snaps should be as close as possible to the top of the vulva. The two half snaps should be placed one above the other with the indentation on the outside of the underpants so that about 2.5 centimetres of cloth separates them. If the cloth of the underpants is thin and likely to tear when you pull at the snaps, a 5 to 7 centimetre strip of cloth can be placed on the inside so that the snaps are connected through both it and the pants. A small piece of adhesive tape over the backs of the snaps will prevent the alarm from sounding as a result of the snaps touching (*see* Fig. 5).

FRONT   VIEW   **BACK   VIEW**

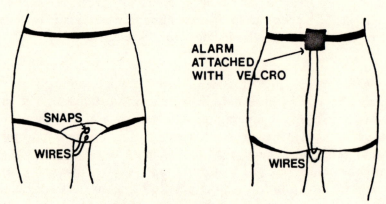

Figure 5. The Pants Alarm in Place

The Toilet Bowl

A second urine alarm is attached to a pot or bowl, which fits snugly in the toilet pan. Ensure that the bottom of the bowl slopes to one side or into the middle when it is placed in the toilet so that urine is likely to run quickly to that side. On that side are placed two moisture-detecting screws that are connected to the alarm by flexible wires.

Connecting the Alarm to the Bowl

Drill two holes at the lowest point in the bottom of the pot or bowl. These holes should be the same size as the screws. They should be placed so that about 2.5 centimetres of the bowl separates them. Place the screws into the holes so that the heads are inside the bowl, then screw the nuts tightly into position. If there appears to be a gap where the screws go through the bowl, smear some epoxy resin around the hole before finally putting the screws in place.

Measure the length of wire required to pass from the alarm, when it is in position behind the toilet, to the screws protruding from the underside of the bowl when it is in the toilet pan. Leave a certain amount of slack in the wires. Cut the wires and strip about 2 centimetres of insulation from the ends. Wrap the end of each wire around one screw, just behind the nut. Solder the wires in place. You can disconnect the wires at any time by placing a hot soldering iron against the solder connection. To test that the connection is complete, pour some water into the bowl so that it covers the screws. The alarm should sound (*see* Fig. 6).

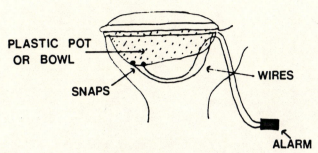

PLASTIC POT
OR BOWL

SNAPS

WIRES

ALARM

Figure 6. The Bowl in Place

Connecting the Snaps to the Pants Alarm

After the wires are in place on the alarm, measure the length required to pass comfortably from the alarm, when it is in position at the waist, to the snaps on the underpants. Leave enough slack to allow an average-sized trainee to bend without straining the wire. A certain amount of slack is acceptable. Take the protruding halves of two snaps. Discard the pin section and solder one snap onto the end of each wire. First cut the wire and strip about 1 centimetre of insulation from the end. Place the end of the wire flat across the back of the snap and solder it on. Test the connection by touching the two snaps together. The alarm should sound. Allow the solder to cool and harden, then clean with a brush and methylated spirits. This will clean the connection of the solder flux so that you can cover it with epoxy resin. The epoxy resin should spread back along the wire and insulation for about 1.5 centimetres beyond the snap. This should prevent the connection from breaking when the alarm is in use.

References

Azrin, N.H., Bugle, C., and O'Brien, F.: Behavioral engineering: two apparatuses for toilet training retarded children. *Journal of Applied Behavior Analysis*, 4:249-253, 1971.

Azrin, N.H., and Foxx, R.M.: A rapid method of toilet training the institutionalized retarded. *Journal of Applied Behavior Analysis*, 4:89-99, 1971.

Madsen, C.H., Hoffman, M., Thomas, D.R., Koropsak, E., and Madsen, C.K.: Comparisons of toilet training techniques. In Gilfand, D.M. (Ed.): *Social Learning in Childhood.* Belmont, California, Brooks/Cole, 1969, pp. 124-132.

Mahoney, K., Van Wagenen, K., and Meyerson, L.: Toilet training of normal and retarded children. *Journal of Applied Behavior Analysis*, 4:173-181, 1971.

Van Wagenen, R.K., Meyerson, L., Kerr, N.J., and Mahoney, K.: Field trials of a new procedure for toilet training. *Journal of Experimental Child Psychology*, 8:147-159, 1969.

Van Wagenen, R.K., and Murdock, E.E.: A transistorized signal package for toilet training of infants. *Journal of Experimental Child Psychology*, 3:312-314, 1966.

Zimmer-Hart, C.L.: An inexpensive, ultra-low current urine alarm. *The Australian Journal of Mental Retardation*, 4:22-24, 1977.

Appendix B
SAMPLE RECORD SHEETS

TOILET TRAINING TO INDEPENDENCE

OBSERVATION RECORD SHEET: DAY

Date: _____

Name of Learner: _____

Names of Observers: _____

Pants checks. Check the learner's pants as unobtrusively as possible every half-hour. Indicate that the check has been made by placing a tick in the appropriate box below.

½ hourly checks	9.00	9.30	10.00	10.30	11.00	11.30	12.00	12.30	1.00	1.30	2.00	2.30	3.00	3.30

Voiding Accidents. Record all voiding accidents below, even if they are discovered between pants checks. Record the time the accident was discovered, and place a tick in the box indicating the size of that accident.

Time:	1	2	3	4	5	6	7	8	9	10
1. Few drops or smear										
2. Small patch on pants										
3. General dampness or partial bowel motion										
4. Few drips or soiling through pants										
5. Large puddle or full bowel motion										

TOILET TRAINING TO INDEPENDENCE

OBSERVATION RECORD SHEET

Toilet voiding. Record all toiletings below. Place a tick beside box 1 for any of the 5 tasks if the learner performed them without prompting or guidance. If prompting and/or guidance were needed describe next to box 2 for the appropriate task. Write in the times of sitting and voiding. Tick in the box provided if learner did not void.

	1	2	3	4	5	6	7	8	9
1. TOILET APPROACH went by self									
2. if helped or directed, describe									
1. PANTS DOWN did by self									
2. if helped or directed describe									
1. SAT ON TOILET did by self									
2. if helped or directed, describe									
Time sat down									
Time voided									
Did not void									
1. STOOD UP did by self									
2. if helped or directed describe									
1. PANTS UP did by self									
2. if helped or directed describe									

Page 1.

TOILET TRAINING TO INDEPENDENCE

PHASE I: PANTS UP: DAY   ☐

Date: _____

Name of Learner: _____

Names of Trainers: _____

TOILETING AIM

The learner pulls up underpants from the knee to the waist without prompts or guidance, while standing with back to the toilet, on 9 trials in a row. You may accept no more than 2 trials which require guidance.

PROCEDURE

Give 3 trials every half hour. Stand learner with back to toilet, pull pants to correct position, give prompt and guidance as required, and reward immediately pants are up to waist level.

Pants Position. Place a tick next to the position being used. Move to the next position after 3 trials without guidance. Cross out each position as it is finished.

1. from hip   2. from buttocks   3. from thigh   4. from knee

Prompts. Place a tick next to the prompt being used. Use prompt 1 until 3 trials without guidance at position have been achieved. Move to the next prompt after 3 trials in a row, without guidance at the previous prompt. Cross out each prompt as it is finished.

1. "John, pants up", raise hand, touch learner's hands.
2. "John, pants up", raise hand, no touch.
3. "Pants up", raise hand.
4. "Up", raise hand.
5. "Raise hand.
6. Raise fingers.
7. Hold hand ready for gesture, no gesture.
8. No prompt.

Toilet voiding and accidents. Record time of toilet use and voiding accidents below. Tick the appropriate box for fully self-initiated toilet use or no voiding.

	1	2	3	4	5	6	7	8	9	10	11	12
Time of toileting												
Toileting self-initiated												
Did not void												
Time of accident												

TOILET TRAINING TO INDEPENDENCE

PHASE I: PANTS UP

Recording. Write in the time each training session started, the pants position, prompt, and the reward used. Tick the box next to the amount of guidance needed for each trial. The guidance recorded is that needed for pants up. Under each session you will have 3 ticks, one for each trial.

HALF-HOURLY SESSION	1	2	3	4	5	6	7
Time started							
Pants position							
Prompt number							
Full guidance							
Half guidance							
Little guidance							
No guidance							
Reward used							

HALF-HOURLY SESSION	8	9	10	11	12	13	14
Time started							
Pants position							
Prompt number							
Full guidance							
Half guidance							
Little guidance							
No guidance							
Reward used							

Comments:

Page 1

TOILET TRAINING TO INDEPENDENCE

PHASE 2: STANDING FROM THE TOILET: DAY

Date: _____

Name of Learner: _____

Names of Trainers: _____

TOILETING AIM

The learner stands up from a sitting position on the toilet and pulls underpants up from the knee to the waist, without prompts or guidance, on 9 trials in a row. You may accept no more than 2 trials which require guidance.

PROCEDURE

Give 3 trials every half hour. Pull the learner's pants to knee level and seat on toilet. Give prompt and guidance as required, and reward immediately pants are up to waist level.

Prompts. Place a tick next to the prompt being used. Move to the next prompt after 3 trials in a row without guidance at the previous prompt. Cross out each prompt as it is finished.

1. "John, stand", raise hand, touch learner's back.
2. "John, stand", raise hand, no touch.
3. "Stand", raise hand.
4. Raise hand.
5. Raise fingers.
6. Hand ready for gesture, no gesture.
7. No prompt.

Toilet voiding and accidents. Record time of toilet use and voiding accidents below. Tick the appropriate box for fully self-initiated toilet use or no voiding.

	1	2	3	4	5	6	7	8	9	10	11	12
Time of toileting												
Toileting self-initiated												
Did not void												
Time of accident												

TOILET TRAINING TO INDEPENDENCE

PHASE 2: STANDING FROM THE TOILET

Recording: Write in the time each training session started, the prompt and the reward used. Tick the box next to the amount of guidance needed for each trial. The guidance recorded is that needed for standing from the toilet. Under each session you will have 3 ticks, one for each trial.

HALF-HOURLY SESSION	1	2	3	4	5	6	7
Time started							
Prompt number							
Full guidance							
Half guidance							
Little guidance							
No guidance							
Reward used							

HALF-HOURLY SESSION	8	9	10	11	12	13	14
Time started							
Prompt number							
Full guidance							
Half guidance							
Little guidance							
No guidance							
Reward used							

Comments:

TOLET TRAINING TO INDEPENDENCE   Page 1.

PHASE 3: VOIDING IN TOILET: DAY [ ]

<u>Date:</u> _____

Name of learner: _____   Names of Trainers: _____

TOILETING AIM

The learner sits quietly after being placed on the toilet, voids in the toilet and stands when finished, without guidance, on 10 voidings in a row. You may accept no more than 2 trials with no toilet voiding or which require guidance.

PROCEDURE

Offer drinks every half-hour. Learner to wear pants alarm and sit on chair in front of toilet with toilet alarm in position. On the sounding of the pants alarm, say "NO" loudly and sharply. Quickly take the learner to the toilet, pull pants to the knee and seat on toilet in correct position. Learner to sit until voiding occurs, or for 20 minutes, whichever is the shortest. Give guidance as required, and reward immediately pants are up to waist level. Do not reward if no voiding occurred.

<u>Drinks:</u> Record time drinks offered and number of cups consumed.

Time drinks offered															
Amount drunk															

Comments: _____

TOILET TRAINING TO INDEPENDENCE

PHASE 3: VOIDING IN TOILET

Page 2.

Recording: Write in below the time of the voiding accident, when seated and voided, the reward used and, if no toilet voiding occurred, the time the learner rose from the toilet. Tick the appropriate box next to the size of accident, and the amount of guidance needed for each trial. The guidance recorded is that needed to remain seated on the toilet. If toileting is fully self-initiated with no accident, write SI above that trial.

TOILETING TRIAL	1	2	3	4	5	6	7	8	9	10	11	12	13	14	15	16
Time learner seated on toilet																
Full guidance																
Half guidance																
Little guidance																
No guidance																
Time voided																
If no voiding Time rose from toilet																
Reward used																
ACCIDENT TIME																
1. Few drops or smear																
2. Small patch on pants																
3. General Dampness or partial bowel motion																
4. Few drips or soiling through pants																
5. Large puddle or full bowel motion																

TOILET TRAINING TO INDEPENDENCE

PHASE 4: SEATING SELF ON TOILET: DAY

Date: _____

Name of Learner: _____   Names of Trainers: _____

TOILETING AIM

The learner seats self in the appropriate position, after being taken to the toilet and having pants pulled down, and voids in toilet without prompts or guidance, on 10 voidings in a row. You may accept no more that 2 trials with no voiding, or which require guidance for seating self.

PROCEDURE

Offer drinks every half hour. Learner to wear pants alarm and sit on chair in front of toilet with toilet alarm in position. On the sounding of the pants alarm, say "NO" loudly and sharply. Quickly take the learner to the toilet, pull pants to the knee and give prompt and guidance as required. Learner to sit until voiding occurs, or for 20 minutes, whichever is the shortest. Reward immediately pants are up to waist level. Do <u>not</u> reward if no voiding occurred.

<u>Prompts</u>. Place a tick next to the prompt being used. Move to the next prompt after 3 trials in a row without guidance at the previous prompt. Cross out each prompt as it is finished.

1. "John, sit", lower hand, touch learner's back.
2. "John, sit" lower hand, no touch.
3. "Sit", lower hand.
4. Lower hand.
5. Lower fingers.
6. Hand ready for gesture, no gesture.
7. No prompt.

<u>Drinks</u>. Record time drinks offered and number of cups consumed.

Time drinks offered										
Amount drunk										

Comments: _____

TOILET TRAINING TO INDEPENDENCE

PHASE 4: SEATING SELF ON TOILET

Recording: Write in below the time of the voiding accident, when seated and voided, the prompt number, the reward used, and, if no toilet voiding occurred, the time the learner rose from the toilet. Tick the appropriate box next to the size of accident, and the amount of guidance needed for each trial. The guidance recorded is that needed to seat self in the correct position. If toileting is fully self-initiated, with no accident, write SI above that trial

TOILETING TRIAL	1	2	3	4	5	6	7	8	9	10	11	12	13	14	15	16
Prompt number																
Full guidance																
Half guidance																
Little guidance																
No guidance																
Time learner seated on toilet																
Time voided																
If no voiding time rose from toilet																
Reward used																
ACCIDENT TIME																
1. Few drops or smear																
2. Small patch on pants																
3. General dampness of partial bowel motion																
4. Few drips or soiling through pants																
5. Large puddle or full bowel motion																

TOILET TRAINING TO INDEPENDENCE

PHASE 5: PANTS DOWN: DAY

Date: _____

Name of Learner: _____   Names of Trainers: _____

TOILETING AIM

The learner pulls pants down after being taken to the toilet, seats self in the appropriate position and voids in the toilet, without prompts or guidance, on 10 voidings in a row. You may accept no more than 2 trials with no voiding, or which require guidance for pants down.

PROCEDURE

Offer drinks every half hour. Learner to wear pants alarm and sit on chair in front of toilet with toilet alarm in position. On the sounding of the pants alarm, say "NO" loudly and sharply. Quickly take the learner to the toilet, stand him with back to toilet, pull pants to correct position, and give prompt and guidance as required. Learner to sit until voiding occurs, or for 20 minutes, whichever is the shortest. Reward immediately pants are up to waist level. Do not reward if no voiding occurred.

Pants position. Place a tick next to the position being used. Move to the next position after 3 trials without guidance. Cross out each position as it is finished.

1. from thigh.   2. from buttocks.   3 from hip.   4. from waist.

Prompts. Place a tick next to the prompt being used. Use prompt 1 until 3 trials without guidance at position 4 have been achieved. Move to the next prompt after 3 trials in a row without guidance at the previous prompt. Cross out each prompt as it is finished.

1. "John, pants down", lower hand, touch learner's hands.
2. "John, pants down", lower hand, no touch.
3. "Pants down", lower hand.
4. "Down", lower hand.
5. Lower hand.
6. Lower fingers.
7. Hand ready for gesture, no gesture.
8. No prompt.

Drinks. Record time drinks offered and number of cups consumed.

Time drinks offered												
Amount drunk												

Comments:

TOILET TRAINING TO INDEPENDENCE

PHASE 5: PANTS DOWN

Recording: Write in below the time of the voiding accident, when seated and voided, pants position and prompt number, the reward used, and, if no toilet voiding occurred, the time the learner rose from the toilet. Tick the appropriate box next to the size of accident, and the amount of guidance needed for each trial. The guidance recorded is that needed for pants down. If toileting is fully self-initiated, with no accident, write SI above that trial.

TOILETING TRIAL	1	2	3	4	5	6	7	8	9	10	11	12	13	14	15	16
Pants position																
Prompt number																
Full guidance																
Half guidance																
Little guidance																
No guidance																
Time learner seated on toilet																
Time voided																
If no voiding Time rose from toilet																
Reward used																
ACCIDENT TIME																
1. Few drops or smear																
2. Small patch on pants																
3. General dampness or partial bowel motion																
4. Few drips or soiling through pants																
5. Large puddle or full bowel motion																

Page 1.

TOILET TRAINING TO INDEPENDENCE

PHASE 6: TOILET APPROACH: DAY

Date:

Name of Learner: Names of Trainers:

TOILETING AIM

The learner stands and walks to the toilet, pulls pants down, sits and voids in the toilet, without having an accident and without prompts or guidance, on 10 voidings in a row. You may accept no more than 2 trials with either accidents or no voiding, or which require guidance for toilet approach.

PROCEDURE

Offer drinks every half hour. Learner to wear pants alarm and sit on chair in front of toilet with toilet alarm in position. On the sounding of the pants alarm, say "NO" loudly and sharply. Give prompt and guidance as required. Learner to sit until voiding occurs, or for 20 minutes, whichever is the shortest. Reward immediately pants are up to waist level. Do not reward if no voiding occurred.

Prompts: Place a tick next to the prompt being used. Move to the next prompt after 3 trials in a row without guidance at the previous prompt. Cross out each prompt as it is finished.

1. "John toilet", point to toilet, touch learner's back.
2. "John toilet", point to toilet, no touch.
3. "Toilet", point to toilet.
4. Point to toilet.
5. Point finger at toilet.
6. Hand ready for gesture, no gesture.
7. No prompt.

Drinks: Record time drinks offered and number of cups consumed.

Time drinks offered													
Amount drunk													

Comments:

TOILET TRAINING TO INDEPENDENCE

PHASE 6: TOILET APPROACH

Recording: Write in below the time of the voiding accident, when seated and voided, prompt number, the reward used, and, if no toilet voiding occurred, the time the learner rose from the toilet. Tick the appropriate box next to the size of accident, and the amount of guidance needed for each trial. The guidance recorded is that needed for toilet approach. If toileting is fully self-initiated, with no accident, write SI above that trial.

TOILETING TRIAL	1	2	3	4	5	6	7	8	9	10	11	12	13	14	15	16
Prompt number																
Full guidance																
Half guidance																
Little guidance																
No guidance																
Time learner seated on toilet																
Time voided																
If no voiding Time rose from toilet																
Reward used																
ACCIDENT TIME																
1. Few drops or smear																
2. Small patch on pants																
3. General dampness or partial bowel motion.																
4. Large puddle or full bowel motion																

Page 1.

TOILET TRAINING TO INDEPENDENCE

PHASE 7: INDEPENDENT TOILETING: DAY ☐

Date: _____

Name of Learner: _____   Names of Trainers: _____

TOILETING AIM

The learner independently toilets self from anywhere in the activity area, without accidents, without prompts or guidance, alarms or extra drinks, and while dressed in normal clothes, on 10 voidings in a row. You may accept no more than 2 trials with either accidents or no voiding, or which require guidance for any part of the toileting sequence.

PROCEDURE

Offer drinks every half hour until Step 6. Learner to be in position according to step reached. Alarms to be in position until Step 7. On the sounding of the pants alarm, or discovery of an accident, say "NO" loudly and sharply. Give minimal guidance necessary. Observe and record all toiletings. Give guidance with normal clothing where necessary at Step 8. Reward immediately pants are up to waist level. Do not reward if no voiding occurred.

Steps. Place a tick next to the step being used. Move to the next step after 3 voiding trials in a row, without accidents, and without guidance. Cross out each step as it is finished.

1. Seated 2 feet from toilet.
2. Seated 4 feet from toilet.
3. Seated 6 feet from toilet.
4. Seated just out of sight of toilet.
5. Free activity in any part of activity area.
6. Free activity in any part of activity area without extra drinks.
7. Free activity in any part of activity area without pants or toilet alarms.
8. Free activity in any part of activity area and dressed in normal clothes.

Drinks: Record time drinks offered and number of cups consumed. Cross out this section from Step 6.

Time drinks offered											
Amount drunk											

Comments:

TOILET TRAINING TO INDEPENDENCE

PHASE 7: INDEPENDENT TOILETING

Recording: Write in below the time of voiding accidents, when seated and voided, step number, reward used, and, if no toileting voiding occurred, the time the learner rose from the toilet. Tick the appropriate box next to the size of accident. Record each fully self-initiated toileting by writing SI above that trial.

TOILETING TRIAL	1	2	3	4	5	6	7	8	9	10	11	12	13	14	15	16
Step number																
Time learner seated on toilet																
Time voided																
If no voiding Time rose from toilet																
Reward used																
IF ACCIDENT Time																
1. Few drops or smear																
2. Small patch on pants																
3. General dampness or partial bowel motion																
4. Few drips or soiling through pants																
5. Large puddle or full bowel motion																

Appendix C
MAINTENANCE INSTRUCTIONS
AND RECORD SHEETS

MAINTENANCE INSTRUCTIONS AND RECORD SHEETS

Date:_____   Name of learner:_____

TOILETING AIM

That _____ toilets him/herself without accidents and without help in the normal environment for 14 days in a row.

Now that_____has learned to look after his/her own toileting, he/she still needs some help from you until this new learning is fully established as a permanent part of life._____may have a few accidents until he/she is sure that everyone expects independent toileting.

ENVIRONMENT

_____ should be involved in whatever activities and routines take place in his/her usual lifestyle. No special routines or activities are necessary. He/she can be at home, at school, at work, visiting, on outings, or on holidays. You will help him/her transfer the new toileting skills to every situation.

SUPERVISION

The trainer(s) will visit and/or telephone you regularly to check progress, discuss problems, and renew your record sheets. Feel free to ring or call the trainer(s) at any time. They are just as concerned as you are that_____transfers the new toileting skills.

DO'S AND DONT'S

1. DO NOT tell or prompt_____to go to the toilet. He/she learns from the accident procedure. If you direct him/her to the toilet, he/she will wait for your reminder and lose independence. If you take other children to the bathroom,_____may go too, but do not direct him/her to the toilet in any other way.

2. DO NOT worry if_____does not go to the toilet when you think he/she may need to. He/she can hold on for a long time.

3. DO make sure that_____has free access to the toilet at all times. If he/she is in an unfamiliar place, show him/her where the toilet is.

4. DO make sure that_____always wears clothing which he/she can easily manage alone when toileting.

5. DO record every pants check, toileting, and accident on the record sheets provided. This will tell you at a glance whether_____is improving.

6. DO contact the trainer(s)_____at_____on number_____if there are any problems or the number of accidents is increasing.

7. YOU MAY tell_____to go to the toilet before an outing if you know that he/she will have no access to toilets for 2 hours or more.

PROCEDURE

Pants checks.

Check whether_____'s pants are dry and clean before each meal, before mid-morning and mid-afternoon drinks (or at the end of school), and before bed. Get_____to feel his/her pants with you. If he/she is dry and clean give a big hug and say how pleased you are.
Do this with enthusiasm. It is a big achievement.
Record the pants checks in the spaces provided at the top of Sheet 1.

Toileting.

Watch_____closely. If he/she goes towards the toilet or pot, follow at a distance and do not interfere. If he/she uses the toilet, wait until the pants are up to waist level, and then praise him/her enthusiastically. Record each toileting in the spaces provided on Sheet 1.

Accidents.

If you discover _____ wet or dirty, say "NO" loudly and sharply and point him/her to the toilet. *Do not* say anything else. *Do not* touch _____ unless he/she does not carry out any one of the toileting tasks correctly. Then only give the least possible point or touch to correct him/her. Once _____ is seated on the toilet keep him/her there for 10–15 minutes. If he/she does not remain seated quietly use a touch or point. Do not look at, touch or talk to him/her in any other way. Do not praise toilet use after an accident.

Record each accident in the space provided on Sheet 1. Record the total number of accidents for each day on Sheet 2.

Note.

Accidents include a small wet or dirty patch on the pants, and any urine or faeces on the toilet seat or on the floor or furniture.

TOILET TRAINING TO INDEPENDENCE

MAINTENANCE RECORD SHEET 1.

Date: _____ Name of Learner: _____ Names of Trainers:

_____

_____

_____

Pants Checks: Place a tick in the six places below when you give each check.

Give praise and affection if dry and clean.

Before breakfast check	Mid-morning snack check	Before lunch check	Mid-afternoon snack check	Before tea check	Before bed check
_____	_____	_____	_____	_____	_____

Toileting: Write in time. Tick the appropriate boxes and initial when finished.

Time went to toilet	No direction was given	Direction was given	Used the toilet	Did not use the toilet	You gave praise & reward	Initial when completed

Accidents: Write in time. Tick the appropriate boxes, and initial when finished. Place an asterisk * beside unavoidable accidents. Note when accident is a bowel movement under comments.

Time found out	Changed pants	Did not talk	Said no sharply	Sat for 10-15 minutes	Any comments	Initial when Complete

Comments:

TOILET TRAINING TO INDEPENDENCE

MAINTENANCE RECORD SHEET 2

Name of Learner:

1. Under the appropriate day record the number of accidents which occurred on that day. If none were detected, record a zero.

2. Do not record accidents which were marked as unavoidable on the Maintenance Record Sheet 1.

DAY

Month	1	2	3	4	5	6	7	8	9	10	11	12	13	14	15	16	17	18	19	20	21	22	23	24	25	26	27	28	29	30	31	Total accidents for month

Appendix D
EXAMPLES OF RECORDING

In this section are included examples showing the method of recording. Instructions for converting the record for graphing purposes may be seen in Appendix E.

TOILET TRAINING TO INDEPENDENCE

OBSERVATION RECORD SHEET: DAY [2]

Date: 5.10.79

Name of Learner: JANE SMITH

Names of Observers: Brenda
Jackie

Pants checks. Check the learner's pants as unobtrusively as possible every half-hour. Indicate that the check has been made by placing a tick in the appropriate box below.

½ hourly checks	9.00	9.30	10.00	10.30	11.00	11.30	12.00	12.30	1.00	1.30	2.00	2.30	3.00	3.30
			✓						✓	✓	✓	✓	✓	✓

Voiding Accidents. Record all voiding accidents below, even if they are discovered between pants checks. Record the time the accident was discovered, and place a tick in the box indicating the size of that accident.

	1	2	3	4	5	6	7	8	9	10
Time	11.30	12.05								
1. Few drops or smear										
2. Small patch on pants										
3. General dampness or partial bowel motion										
4. Few drips or soiling through pants	✓									
5. Large puddle or full bowel motion		✓								

TOILET TRAINING TO INDEPENDENCE

OBSERVATION RECORD SHEET

Toilet voiding. Record all toiletings below. Place a tick beside box 1 for any of the 5 tasks if the learner performed them without prompting or guidance. If prompting and/or guidance were needed describe next to box 2 for the appropriate task. Write in the times of sitting and voiding. Tick in the box provided if learner did not void.

	1	2	3	4	5	6	7	8	9
1. TOILET APPROACH went by self	Taken full guidance ↓								
2. if helped or directed, describe		Toilet sign (gestural prompt	Toilet sign (gestural prompt						
1. PANTS DOWN did by self	full guidance	✓	✓						
2. if helped or directed describe									
1. SAT ON TOILET did by self	✓	✓	✓						
2. if helped or directed, describe									
Time sat down	9.04	10.25	1.55						
Time voided	immediate	immediate	immediate						
Did not void									
1. STOOD UP did by self	✓			Pull pants up In front & needed help at back and front to complete					
2. if helped or directed describe		verbal prompt & touch on arm	little guidance	↗ after some put hand in toilet to play					
1. PANTS UP did by self									
2. if helped or directed describe	full guidance	self guidance	half guidance						

TOILET TRAINING TO INDEPENDENCE

Page 1.

PHASE I: PANTS UP: DAY [1]

Date: 29.10.79

Name of Learner: Jear Smith   Names of Trainers: Sue, Pat, Clark, Brooks

TOILETING AIM

The learner pulls up underpants from the knee to the waist without prompts or guidance, while standing with back to the toilet, on 9 trials in a row. You may accept no more than 2 trials which require guidance.

PROCEDURE

Give 3 trials every half hour. Stand learner with back to toilet, pull pants to correct position, give prompt and guidance as required, and reward immediately pants are up to waist level.

Pants Position. Place a tick next to the position being used. Move to the next position after 3 trials without guidance. Cross out each position as it is finished.
1. from hip   2. from buttocks   3. from thigh   4. from knee

Prompts. Place a tick next to the prompt being used. Use prompt 1 until 3 trials without guidance at position have been achieved. Move to the next prompt after 3 trials in a row, without guidance at the previous prompt. Cross out each prompt as it is finished.

1. "John, pants up", raise hand, touch learner's hands. ✓
2. "John, pants up", raise hand, no touch.
3. "Pants up", raise hand.
4. "Up", raise hand.
5. Raise hand.
6. Raise fingers.
7. Hold hand ready for gesture, no gesture.
8. No prompt.

Toilet voiding and accidents. Record time of toilet use and voiding accidents below.
Tick the appropriate box for fully self-initiated toilet use or no voiding.

	1	2	3	4	5	6	7	8	9	10	11	12
Time of toileting	9.25			1.14	2.03	3.08						
Toileting self-initiated												
Did not void												
Time of accident	9.25	10.30	11.29	1.14								

TOILET TRAINING TO INDEPENDENCE

PHASE I: PANTS UP

Recording. Write in the time each training session started, the pants position, prompt, and the reward used. Tick the box next to the amount of guidance needed for each trial. The guidance recorded is that needed for pants up. Under each session you will have 3 ticks, one for each trial.

HALF-HOURLY SESSION	1	2	3	4	5	6	7
Time started	9.00	9.35	10.00	10.30	11.00	11.30	12.00
Pants position	-	-	-	-	-	-	-
Prompt number	1	1	1	1	1	1	1
Full guidance	✓✓	✓	✓	✓			✓
Half guidance	✓	✓	✓	✓		✓	✓✓
Little guidance	✓		✓	✓	✓✓		
No guidance		✓✓	✓		✓✓		
Reward used	beads T.V	beads T.V	beads Train	beads	beads Music	Music Train	music

HALF-HOURLY SESSION	8	9	10	11	12	13	14
Time started	12.30	1.00	1.30	2.00	2.30	3.00	3.30
Pants position	1	1	1	1	1	1	2
Prompt number	1	1	1	1	1	1	1
Full guidance			✓				
Half guidance	✓✓	✓	✓	✓✓	✓		
Little guidance	✓	✓	✓	✓✓	✓✓	✓✓	✓✓
No guidance		✓				✓✓✓	✓
Reward used	music	music	music	music	music	music	music

Comments: Prefers Music Box. Throws beads away.

Page 1

TOILET TRAINING TO INDEPENDENCE

PHASE 2: STANDING FROM THE TOILET: DAY [4]

Date: 11. 11. 79   Name of Learner: Jane Smith   Names of Trainers: Jenny, Sue, Tony, Mac

TOILETING AIM

The learner stands up from a sitting position on the toilet and pulls underpants up from the knee to the waist, without prompts or guidance, on 9 trials in a row. You may accept no more than 2 trials which require guidance.

PROCEDURE

Give 3 trials every half hour. Pull the learner's pants to the knee level and seat on toilet. Give prompt and guidance as required, and reward immediately pants are up to waist level.

Prompts. Place a tick next to the prompt being used. Move to the next prompt after 3 trials in a row without guidance at the previous prompt. Cross out each prompt as it is finished.

1. "John, stand", raise hand, touch learner's back. ✓
2. "John, stand", raise hand, no touch. ✓
3. "Stand", raise hand. ✓
4. Raise hand. ✓
5. Raise finger. ✓
6. Hand ready for gesture, no gesture.
7. No prompt.

Toilet voiding and accidents. Record time of toilet use and voiding accidents below. Tick the appropriate box for fully self-initiated toilet use or no voiding.

	1	2	3	4	5	6	7	8	9	10	11	12
Time of toileting		12.35		2.05	2.36	3.28						
Toileting self-initiated												
Did not void						✓						
Time of accident	12.28		2.16									

Page 2

TOILET TRAINING TO INDEPENDENCE

PHASE 2: STANDING FROM THE TOILET

Recording: Write in the time each training session started, the prompt and the reward used. Tick the box next to the amount of guidance needed for each trial. The guidance recorded is that needed for standing from the toilet. Under each session you will have 3 ticks, one for each trial.

HALF-HOURLY SESSION	1	2	3	4	5	6	7
Time started	9:00	9:30	10:00	10:30	11:00	11:30	12:00
Prompt number	1	1	1	1	1	2	3
Full guidance							
Half guidance	✓						
Little guidance	✓✓	✓✓	✓	✓✓			✓✓
No guidance		✓	✓✓		✓✓✓	✓✓✓	✓
Reward used	music	music	music	music	Praise hugs	Praise hugs	music

HALF-HOURLY SESSION	8	9	10	11	12	13	14
Time started	12:30	1:00	1:30	2:00	2:30	3:00	3:30
Prompt number	3	3	4	5	5	5	5
Full guidance							
Half guidance							
Little guidance	✓✓✓		✓	✓	✓	✓	✓
No guidance		✓✓✓	✓✓	✓	✓	✓	✓✓
Reward used	music	music	Praise hugs	Praise hugs	wiggle	wiggle	waggle.

Comments:

TOILET TRAINING TO INDEPENDENCE

Page 1.

PHASE 3: VOIDING IN TOILET: DAY 6

Date: 5.11.79

Name of learner: Jean Smith

Names of Trainers: Rot, Jenny / Sue

TOILETING AIM

The learner sits quietly after being placed on the toilet, voids in the toilet and stands when finished, without guidance, on 10 voidings in a row. You may accept no more than 2 trials with no toilet voiding or which require guidance.

PROCEDURE

Offer drinks every half-hour. Learner to wear pants alarm and sit on chair in front of toilet with toilet alarm in position. On the sounding of the pants alarm, say "NO" loudly and sharply. Quickly take the learner to the toilet, pull pants to the knee and seat on toilet in correct position. Learner to sit until voiding occurs, or for 20 minutes, whichever is the shortest. Give guidance as required, and reward immediately pants are up to waist level. Do not reward if no voiding occurred.

Drinks: Record time drinks offered and number of cups consumed.

Time drinks offered	9.05	9.30	10.00	10.30	11.00	11.30	12.00	12.30	1.00	1.30	2.00	2.30	3.00
Amount drunk	1	1	1	1	3/4	1	1	1	3/4	2½	3/4	½	

Comments:

TOILET TRAINING TO INDEPENDENCE

PHASE 3: VOIDING IN TOILET

Recording: Write in below the time of the voiding accident, when seated and voided, the reward used, if no toilet voiding occurred, the time the learner rose from the toilet. Tick the appropriate box next to the size of accident, and the amount of guidance needed for each trial. The guidance recorded is that needed to remain seated on the toilet. If toileting is fully self-initiated with no accident, write SI above that trial.

TOILETING TRIAL	1	2	3	4	5	6	7	8	9	10	11	12	13	14	15	16
Time learner seated on toilet	10:52	11:47	12:14	1:40	2:42											
Full guidance																
Half guidance																
Little guidance	✓	✓			✓											
No guidance			✓	✓		✓										
Time voided	10:55	immed	immed	immed	immed	immed										
If no voiding Time rose from toilet																
Reward used	most music	music	music	music	music	music										
ACCIDENT TIME	10:52	11:47	12:15		10b	2:42										
1. Few drops or smear			✓													
2. Small patch on pants	✓				✓											
3. General Dampness or partial bowel motion																
4. Few drips or soiling through pants																
5. Large puddle or full bowel motion		✓				✓										

TOILET TRAINING TO INDEPENDENCE
PHASE 4: SEATING SELF ON TOILET: DAY [8]

Date: 7.11.79

Name of Learner: Jane Smith

Names of Trainers: Roxy Sue

Mrs Smith

TOILETING AIM

The learner seats self in the appropriate position, after being taken to the toilet and having pants pulled down, and voids in toilet without prompts or guidance, on 10 voidings in a row. You may accept no more than 2 trials with no voiding, or which require guidance for seating self.

PROCEDURE

Offer drinks every half hour. Learner to wear pants alarm. Learner to be taken to the toilet with toilet alarm in position. On the sounding of the pants alarm, say "NO" loudly and sharply. Quickly take the learner to the toilet, pull pants to the knee and give prompt and guidance as required. Learner to sit until voiding occurs, or for 20 minutes, whichever is the shortest. Reward immediately pants are up to waist level. Do not reward if no voiding occurred.

Prompts. Place a tick next to the prompt being used. Move to the next prompt after 3 trials in a row without guidance at the previous prompt. Cross out each prompt as it is finished.

1. "John, sit", lower hand, touch learner's back. ✓
2. "John, sit" lower hand, no touch ✓
3. "Sit", lower hand. ✓
4. Lower hand.
5. Lower fingers.
6. Hand ready for gesture, no gesture.
7. No prompt.

Drinks. Record time drinks offered and number of cups consumed.

Time drinks offered	9.00	9.30	10.00	10.30	11.00	11.30	12.00	12.30	1.00	1.30	2.00	2.30	3.00		
Amount drunk	2	1¾	2½	2¾	1½	2	1	1	1½	1½	½	¼			

Comments:

TOILET TRAINING TO INDEPENDENCE

PHASE 4: SEATING SELF ON TOILET

Recording: Write in below the time of the voiding accident, when seated and voided, the prompt number, the reward used, and, if no toilet voiding occurred, the time the learner rose from the toilet. Tick the appropriate box next to the size of accident, and the amount of guidance needed for each trial. The guidance recorded is that needed to seat self in the correct position. If toileting is fully self-initiated, with no accident, write SI above that trial.

TOILETING TRIAL	1	2	3	4	5	6	7	8	9	10	11	12	13	14	15	16
Prompt number	1	1	1	1	1	2	2	2	3 SI	3	3	3	3			
Full guidance																
Half guidance																
Little guidance	✓															
No guidance		✓	✓	✓	✓	✓	✓	✓	✓	✓	✓	✓				
Time learner seated on toilet	9·29	10·03	10·43	10·53	11·24	11·30	12·09	11·40	1·41	2·00	2·45	3·25				
Time voided					1 min											
If no voiding time rose from toilet																
Reward used																
ACCIDENT TIME	9·39	10·03	10·43	10·50	11·24	11·30	12·09	12·40		2·00	2·45					
1. Few drops or smear		✓		✓												
2. Small patch on pants																
3. General dampness of partial bowel motion			✓			✓										
4. Few drips or soiling through pants										✓						
5. Large puddle or full bowel motion	✓				✓		✓				✓					

TOILET TRAINING TO INDEPENDENCE
PHASE 5: PANTS DOWN: DAY [23]

Date: 20.7.79.

Name of Learner: John Downs

Names of Trainers: Sus, Terry

TOILETING AIM

The learner pulls pants down after being taken to the toilet, seats self in the appropriate position and voids in position, without prompts or guidance, on 10 voidings in a row. You may accept no more than 2 trials with no voiding, or which require guidance for pants down.

PROCEDURE

Offer drinks every half hour. Learner to wear pants alarm. Learner to sit on chair in front of toilet with toilet alarm in position. On the sounding of the pants alarm, say "NO" loudly and sharply. Quickly take the learner to the toilet, stand him with back to toilet, pull pants to correct position, and give prompt and guidance as required. Learner to sit until voiding occurs, or for 20 minutes, whichever is the shortest. Reward immediately pants are up to waist level. Do not reward if no voiding occurred.

Pants position. Place a tick next to the position being used. Move to the next position after 3 trials without guidance. Cross out each position as it is finished.

1. from thigh. ✚
2. from buttocks
3. from hip
4. from waist ✓

Prompts. Place a tick next to the prompt being used. Use prompt 1 until 3 trials without guidance at position 4 have been achieved. Move to the next prompt after 3 trials in a row without guidance at the previous prompt. Cross out each prompt as it is finished.

1. "John, pants down", lower hand, touch learner's hands. ✚
2. "John, pants down", lower hand, no touch. ✓
3. "Pants down", lower hand. ✓
4. "Down", lower hand.
5. Lower hand.
6. Lower fingers.
7. Hand ready for gesture, no gesture.
8. No prompt.

Drinks. Record time drinks offered and number of cups consumed.

Time drinks offered	9.10	9.35	10.00	10.30	11.00	11.30	12.00	12.30	1.00	1.30	2.00	2.30	3.00		
Amount drunk	1½	1¼	½	1	¾	¾	⅔	⅔	1	⅔	⅔	½	½		

Comments:

TOILET TRAINING TO INDEPENDENCE
PHASE 5: PANTS DOWN

Recording: Write in below the time of the voiding accident, when seated and voided, pants position and prompt number, the reward used, and, if no toilet voiding occurred, the time the learner rose from the toilet. Tick the appropriate box next to the size of accident, and the amount of guidance needed for each trial. The guidance recorded is that needed for pants down. If toileting is fully self-initiated, with no accident, write SI above that trial.

TOILETING TRIAL	1	2	3	4	5	6	7	8	9	10	11	12	13	14	15	16
Pants position	4	4	4	4	4	4	4	4	4							
Prompt number	2	2	2	2	2	2	3	3	3							
Full guidance																
Half guidance																
Little guidance	✓	✓	✓				✓									
No guidance				✓	✓	✓		✓								
Time learner seated on toilet	10:42	11:19	11:54	12:36	1:14	1:19	2:27	3:27								
Time voided	3rd Busta	instead 10sec		general livia	livia	6min	17min finished									
If no voiding Time rose from toilet																
Reward used	chips drops	chips drops	chips doll drops	chips drops	chips choc	choc choc	choc chips sultana	chips sultana								
ACCIDENT TIME	10:42	11:19	11:54	12:36	1:14	1:39	2:27									
1. Few drops or smear																
2. Small patch on pants																
3. General dampness or partial bowel motion			✓	✓		✓										
4. Few drips or soiling through pants					✓		✓									
5. Large puddle or full bowel motion	✓															

TOILET TRAINING TO INDEPENDENCE
PHASE 6: TOILET APPROACH: DAY [30]

Page 1.

Date: 10.8.79

Name of Learner: John Brown

Names of Trainers: Brenda, Sue, Ros, Liz

                                    Jackie

TOILETING AIM

The learner stands and walks to the toilet, pulls pants down, sits and voids in the toilet, without having an accident and without prompts or guidance, on 10 voidings in a row. You may accept no more than 2 trials with either accidents or no voiding, or which require guidance for toilet approach.

PROCEDURE

Offer drinks every half hour. Learner to wear pants alarm and sit on chair in front of toilet with toilet alarm in position. On the sounding of the pants alarm, say "NO" loudly and sharply. Give prompt and guidance as required. Learner to sit until voiding occurs, or for 20 minutes, whichever is the shortest. Reward immediately pants are up to waist level. Do not reward if no voiding occurred.

Prompts: Place a tick next to the prompt being used. Move to the next prompt after 3 trials in a row without guidance at the previous prompt. Cross out each prompt as it is finished.

1. "John toilet", point to toilet, touch learner's back. ✓
2. "John toilet", point to toilet, no touch. ✓
3. "Toilet", point to toilet.
4. Point to toilet.
5. Point finger at toilet.
6. Hand ready for gesture, no gesture.
7. No prompt.

Drinks: Record time drinks offered and number of cups consumed.

Time drinks offered	9:00	9:30	10:00	10:30	11:00	11:30	12:00	12:30	1:00	1:30	2:00	2:30	3:00		
Amount drunk	3	1¼	1	2½	3	1	1	1	2	1½	1½	½	¼		

Comments:

TOILET TRAINING TO INDEPENDENCE
PHASE 6: TOILET APPROACH

Recording: Write in below the time of the voiding accident, when seated and voided, prompt number, the reward used, and, if no toilet voiding occurred, the time the learner rose from the toilet. Tick the appropriate box next to the size of accident, and the amount of guidance needed for each trial. The guidance recorded is that needed for toilet approach. If toileting is fully self-initiated, with no accident, write SI above that trial.

TOILETING TRIAL	1	2	3	4	5	6	7	8	9	10	11	12	13	14	15	16
Prompt number	1	1	2	2	2	2	3									
Full guidance																
Half guidance																
Little guidance			✓													
No guidance	✓	✓		✓	✓	✓										
Time learner seated on toilet	11.15	11.46	1.16	2.35	2.45	3.20										
Time voided	passed 18min	incomes immed 6min arranged														
If no voiding Time rose from toilet																
Reward used	choc	choc	chips	choc	chips	chips										
ACCIDENT TIME	11.35	11.46	1.16	2.35	2.45	3.20										
1. Few drops or smear		✓														
2. Small patch on pants					✓	✓										
3. General dampness or partial bowel motion				✓	✓											
4. Large puddle or full bowel motion	✓		✓	✓												

TOILET TRAINING TO INDEPENDENCE
PHASE 7: INDEPENDENT TOILETING: DAY [13]

Page 1.

Date: 14.11.79   Name of Learner: Jane Smith   Names of Trainers: Rox, Sue, Janny

Tony

TOILETING AIM

The learner independently toilets self from anywhere in the activity area, without accidents, without prompts or guidance, alarms or extra drinks, and while dressed in normal clothes, on 10 voidings in a row. You may accept no more than 2 trials with either accidents or no voiding, or which require guidance for any part of the toileting sequence.

387 4055.

PROCEDURE

Offer drinks every half hour until Step 6. Learner to be in position according to step reached. Alarms to be in position until Step 7. On the sounding of the pants alarm, or discovery of an accident, say "NO" loudly and sharply. Give minimal guidance necessary. Observe and record all toiletings. Give guidance with normal clothing where necessary at Step 8. Reward immediately pants are up to waist level. Do not reward if no voiding occurred.

Steps. Place a tick next to the step being used. Move to the next step after 3 voiding trials in a row, without accidents, and without guidance. Cross out each step as it is finished.

1. Seated 2 feet from toilet.
2. Seated 4 feet from toilet.
3. Seated 6 feet from toilet.
4. Seated just out of sight of toilet. ✓
5. Free activity in any part of activity area. ✓
6. Free activity in any part of activity area without extra drinks.
7. Free activity in any part of activity area without pants or toilet alarms.
8. Free activity in any part of activity area and dressed in normal clothes.

Drinks: Record time drinks offered and number of cups consumed. Cross out this section from step 6.

Time drinks offered	9.15	9.45	10.00	10.30	11.00	11.30	12.00	12.30	1.00	1.30	2.00	2.30	3.00		
Amount drunk	2	1¼	2	2	1½	2	2	2	1	2	2	½	¼		

Comments:

TOILET TRAINING TO INDEPENDENCE
PHASE 7:   INDEPENDENT TOILETING

Recording: Write in below the time of voiding accidents, when seated and voided, step number, reward used, and, if no toileting voiding occurred, the time the learner rose from the toilet. Tick the appropriate box next to the size of accident. Record each fully self-initiated toileting by writing SI above that trial.

TOILETING TRIAL	1	2	3	4	5	6	7	8	9	10	11	12	13	14	15	16
Step number	3	4	4	4	4	5	5	5	5							
Time learner seated on toilet	10·17	11·12	11·38	12·05	12·48	12·56	2·02	2·25								
Time voided	immed	immed	immed	immed	immed	immed	immed	immed								
If no voiding Time rose from toilet																
Reward used	music	Music	Music	music	music	bugs	bugs	music								
IF ACCIDENT Time		11·12					2·02	2·25								
1. Few drops or smear																
2. Small patch on pants		✓			alarm had come off and did not sound, prompted not discover it until after toileted SIR		✓									
3. General dampness or partial bowel motion								✓								
4. Few drips or soiling through pants																
5. Large puddle or full bowel motion																

TOILET TRAINING TO INDEPENDENCE

MAINTENANCE RECORD SHEET 1.

Date: 28.12.79   Name of Learner: Jane Smith   Names of Trainers:

Marj Smith

Bill

_____

Pants Checks: Place a tick in the six places below when you give each check.
Give praise and affection if dry and clean.

Before breakfast check	Mid-morning snack check	Before lunch check	Mid-afternoon snack check	Before tea check	Before bed check
✓	✓	✓	✓	✓	✓

Toileting: Write in time. Tick the appropriate boxes and initial when finished.

Time went to toilet	No direction was given	Direction was given	Used the toilet	Did not use the toilet	You gave praise & reward	Initial when complete
7.30 am	✓		✓		✓	ms.
2.10 pm	✓		✓		✓	BS

Accidents: Write in time. Tick the appropriate boxes, and initial when finished. Place an asterisk * beside unavoidable accidents. Note when accident is a bowel movement under comments.

Time found out	Changed pants	Did not talk	Said no sharply	Sat for 10-15 minutes	Any comments	Initial when Completed
2.30	✓	✓	✓	✓	✓	MS

Comments:

TOILET TRAINING TO INDEPENDENCE

MAINTENANCE RECORD SHEET 2

Name of Learner: Jane Smith

1. Under the appropriate day record the number of accidents which occurred on that day. If none were detected, record a zero.

2. Do not record accidents which were marked as unavoidable on the Maintenance Record Sheet 1.

DAY

Month	1	2	3	4	5	6	7	8	9	10	11	12	13	14	15	16	17	18	19	20	21	22	23	24	25	26	27	28	29	30	31	Total accidents for month
November	///	///	///	///	///	///	///	///	///	///	///	///	///	///	///	///	0	0	0	0	0	0	0	0	0	1	0	1	0	0	/	2
December	0	0	0	1	0	0	0	0	1	1	0	0	0	0	0	0	0	0	0	0	0	1	0	0	1	0						5

Appendix E
INSTRUCTIONS FOR GRAPHING

INSTRUCTIONS FOR GRAPHING

Generally, the purpose of a graph is to show at a glance the changes and trends in the measures that have been recorded over a period of time. Consequently, graphs should be clear, simple, and easy to read. Always label every aspect of the graph carefully and include a title, so that anyone reading the graph knows exactly what is being shown.

The units of the measure being graphed are always shown on the vertical axis, and the time over which the measure was taken is shown on the horizontal axis. Allow for all possible values of the measure when deciding on the range of units on the vertical axis. The distance between the units on the two axes should be about the same distance apart to avoid distorting the picture. Make the distance between points far enough apart so that the entries in the graph are not crowded.

One measure per graph provides the clearest picture. However, sometimes it is useful to plot several measures on one graph in order to compare them. When this is done, use different colours or symbols to denote each measure, and provide a key to describe each measure.

Toilet Voiding, Self-Initiated Toilet Use, and Accidents

For each day of observation and training, total the number of toilet voidings, self-initiated toilet uses, and accidents. Enter each of the three totals on the graph(s) at the point where that number on the vertical axis intersects with the day marked on the horizontal axis.

Size of Accidents

The descriptions on the record sheet of the size of accidents have numbers beside them. A few drops or smear is number 1. A large puddle or full-bowel motion is number 5. A tick on the record sheet indicating that an accident is only a few drops is, therefore, given a value of 1, and a tick indicating that the accident caused general dampness is given a value of 3. Total all the ticks for that day.

Example: 1 tick at size 2 = 2
2 ticks at size 3 = 6
2 ticks at size 5 = 10
18

Divide this total by the number of accidents for that day to give an average size of accident.

Example: Total size of accidents = 18
Number of accidents = 5

$$
5 \overline{)18} \quad \text{3.6 (average size of accident)}
$$

15
30
30
0

Enter this average size of accident on the graph at the point where that value on the vertical axis intersects with the day marked on the horizontal axis.

Time Taken to Void in the Toilet

For each toileting, the time of sitting and of the beginning of voiding is recorded. Subtract the first from the second to give the length of time taken to void in the toilet at each toileting.

Example: Time voiding began = 10:33
     Time of sitting = 10:30
     Length of time to ‾‾‾‾‾‾
     void   = 3 minutes

Omit any toiletings at which no voiding occurred. Total the lengths of time for all toilet voidings on that day, and divide by the number of toilet voidings.

Example: Total of lengths of time to void = 10.5 minutes
     Total time in seconds   = 630 seconds
     Number of toilet voidings   = 5

$$\begin{array}{r} 126 \\ 5\overline{)\,630} \\ 500 \\ \overline{130} \\ 100 \\ \overline{30} \\ 30 \\ \overline{0} \end{array}$$

126 seconds, or 2 minutes and 6 seconds average time taken to void in toilet

Enter the average time taken to void in the toilet at the point where that time on the vertical axis intersects with the day marked on the horizontal axis.

Level of Performance on the Five Toileting Tasks

Each of these measures is derived from the record of prompts and guidance entered on the record sheet. Full guidance is assigned a zero. Performance with no prompt or guidance has a value of 5. The values are as follows:

no prompt, no guidance	5
gestural prompt, no guidance	4
verbal prompt, no guidance (with or without a gesture)	3
a little guidance (with or without a prompt)	2
guidance about half the time (with or without a prompt)	1
guidance for approximately the whole task (with or without a prompt)	0

For each trial, assign the correct value by referring to the values above. Total these values for that task for the whole day.

Example 1: Trial 1 — A tick against half guidance   = 1
            Trial 2 — A tick against a little guidance = 2
            Trial 3 — A tick against no guidance on
                Prompt 2 (a verbal prompt)   = 3
                                         Total = 6

Example 2: Trial 1 — A tick against full guidance   = 0
            Trial 2 — A tick against a little guidance = 2
            Trial 3 — A tick against no guidance on
                Prompt 5 (a gestural prompt) = 4
                                         Total = 6

Divide this total by the number of trials on which that task was measured for that day to give an average performance level for that task.

Example: Total performance level = 6
         Number of trials   = 3

$$3\overline{)6} \quad \frac{2}{} \text{ (average performance level)}$$

$$\frac{6}{0}$$

Enter the average performance level on the graph(s) at the point where that number on the vertical axis intersects with the day marked on the horizontal axis.

Appendix F

GRAPHS OF ONE LEARNER'S PERFORMANCE

GRAPHS OF ONE LEARNER'S PERFORMANCE

The following six graphs show the changes in the ten measures of toileting skill recorded on the record sheets. These graphs are taken from the full record of one learner's performance during the testing of this programme. The learner's name is fictitious. Read the following notes as you look at the graphs.

Voiding Accidents: Graph 1.

The number of accidents during the baseline observation period were not stable. However, the number of accidents increased rather than decreased over the seven days. There was no improvement in accident rate.

During Phases 1 and 2 the number of accidents actually decreased, although there was no direct training of toileting or sphincter control during that time. When extra drinks were introduced on day 6, the number of accidents increased markedly and then decreased to below baseline level. This decrease was probably due to an increasing ability to hold back voiding until toileting occurred. The accident rate dropped to zero on the last day of extra drinks and remained at zero for the last three days of training.

NUMBER OF ACCIDENTS DURING BASELINE AND TRAINING

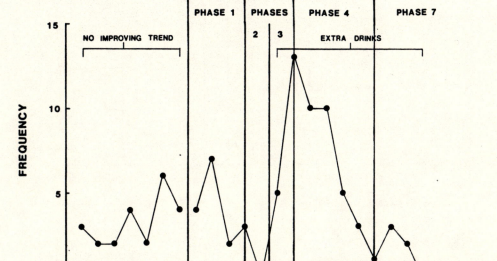

The Size of Accidents: Graph 2.

The size of accidents during the first 4 baseline days indicated that sphincter control to stop voiding accidents did not occur. However, there was some success in stopping voiding accidents during the last three baseline days. Although there was some variation in the average size of accidents during these three days, there was no trend towards increasing sphincter control.

During Phases 1 and 2, the average size of accidents decreased markedly, although there was no direct training of sphincter control during this time. When extra drinks were introduced on day 6, the average size of accidents increased markedly. On the average, accidents were large enough to cause general dampness or drips of urine through the pants until day 14, after which no further accidents occurred.

SIZE OF ACCIDENTS DURING BASELINE AND TRAINING

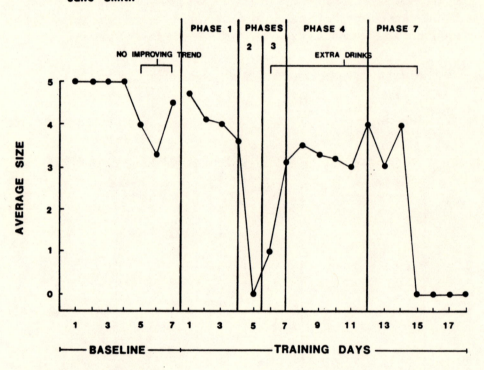

Toilet Voiding: Graph 3.

The number of voidings in the toilet increased slightly during the first three baseline days. However, during the last 4 baseline days, the number of toilet voidings remained stable at between 2 and 3 a day.

During Phases 1 and 2, the number of toilet voidings varied considerably with no apparent trend, although on day 5 the number increased at the same time as the number of accidents decreased. (*see* Graph 1). Once extra drinks and training for toilet use was introduced on day 6, the number of toilet voidings increased markedly, reaching a peak of 14 on day 12. With the beginning of Phase 7, when toileting was mostly self-initiated, the number of toileting voidings gradually decreased. There was a further decrease after day 15 when the extra drinks ceased.

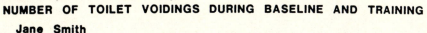

NUMBER OF TOILET VOIDINGS DURING BASELINE AND TRAINING
Jane Smith

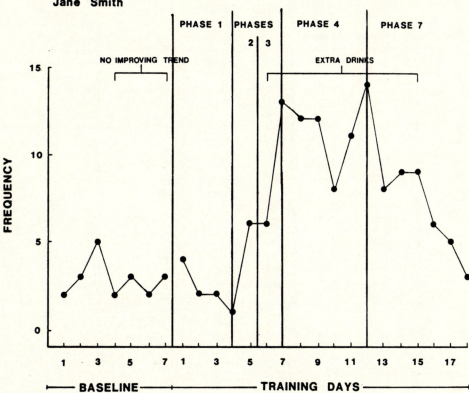

Self-Initiated Toilet Use: Graph 4.

During the baseline observation period, no toiletings were self-initiated There were similarly no self-initiated toiletings during Phases 1 and 2. Once training for toilet use and extra drinks were introduced on day 6, self-initiated toilet voiding began to occur and gradually increased to a peak of 13 on day 12. Once the learner was left to initiate her own toileting in Phase 7, the number of self-initiated toilet voidings decreased. Once the extra drinks ceased, all toiletings were self-initiated (*see* Graph 3) and there were no accidents (*see* Graph 1).

Time Taken to Void in the Toilet: Graph 5.

The ability to voluntarily start voiding immediatly after sitting on the toilet was already in existence before training. Consequently, voiding in the toilet was usually immediate and never more than a minute after sitting, on the average, throughout both the baseline observation period and training.

NUMBER OF SELF-INITIATED TOILET VOIDINGS DURING BASELINE AND TRAINING

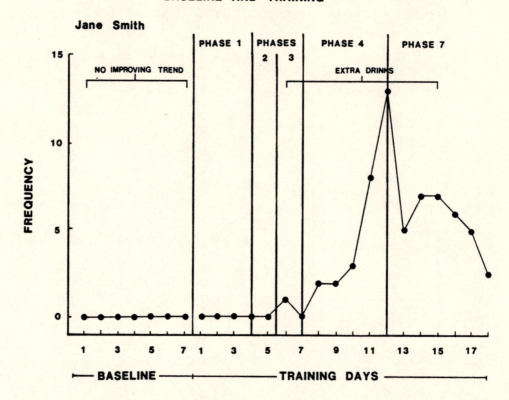

Jane Smith

TIME TAKEN TO VOID IN TOILET DURING BASELINE AND TRAINING

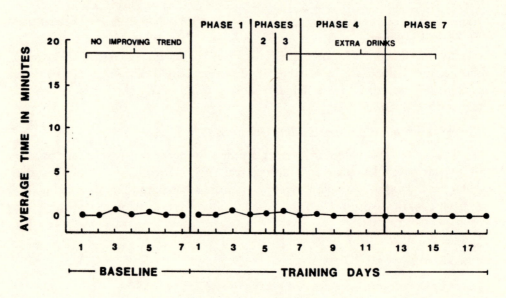

Jane Smith

Level of Performance on Five Toileting Tasks: Graph 6.

Performance on the task, pants up, was the worst, although it improved slightly during the first 3 baseline days. Thereafter, it remained at a low level. It improved considerably over four days of Phase 1, which directly taught this skill. The levels of performance on the graph are an average for the whole day. Consequently, on day 4, when 9 pants-up trials in a row were achieved without prompts or guidance, the point on the graph is below level 5. The average performance for that day included a number of earlier trials when prompts or guidance were required.

Standing up from the toilet varied considerably during the first 3 days of baseline, but then stabilised during the rest of the baseline observation period at the highest level. Phase 2, which taught standing from the toilet, was short because this skill required little training. The average levels on this task during Phase 2 reflect the progress through the prompts required by the programme.

Sitting in the appropriate position on the toilet was not fully achieved on the first baseline day, but was performed at the highest level during the remainder of the baseline observation period. However, the average performance of this skill was poor at the beginning of Phase 4, which taught sitting on the toilet. This was probably due to the stress involved in responding to the loud "no" and holding back voiding that initially interfered with the performance of this task. Performance steadily improved during Phase 4. Self-initiated toileting also increased during this phase (*see* Graph 4). Sitting was always performed perfectly during these toiletings. In fact, the final criterion for this task was not completed because the number of self-initiated toiletings in a row enabled this learner to move directly on to Phase 7.

Pants down and toilet approach did not require training because the learner began to perform these tasks perfectly during all self-initiated toiletings. Pants down varied considerably during the first 4 baseline days. It then stabilised at the highest level for the last 3 baseline days. Toilet approach varied considerably during the baseline observation period, without any tendency to improve.

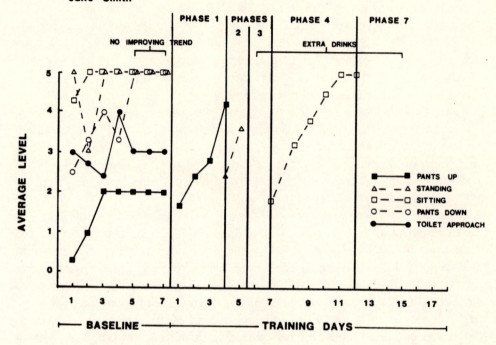

BIBLIOGRAPHY

THESE ARTICLES AND BOOKS MAY BE USEFUL IF YOU are looking for solutions to problems that have arisen during training. They have provided many of the ideas that led to the development of this programme. In particular, Azrin and Mahoney and their associates developed many of the basic procedures upon which this programme is based.

Azrin, N.H., and Foxx, R.M.: A rapid method of toilet training the institutionalized retarded. *Journal of Applied Behavior Analysis, 4*:89-99, 1971.

Baldwin, V.L., Fredericks, H.D. Bud and Brodsky, G.: *Isn't It Time He Outgrew This? or A Training Program for Parents of Retarded Children.* Springfield, Thomas, 1973.

Balthazar, E.E.: *Balthazar Scales of Adaptive Behavior for the Profoundly and Severely Mentally Retarded.* Champaign, Illinois, Research Press, 1971.

Bettison, S.: Toilet training the retarded: Analysis of stages of development and procedures for designing programs. *Australian Journal of Mental Retardation, 5*:95-100, 1978.

Bettison, S.: Toilet training. In Griffin, M.W., and Hudson, A.M. (Eds.): *Children's Problems.* Collingwood, Victoria, Circus Books, 1979.

Bettison, S.: Daytime wetting and soiling. In Hudson, A.M., and Griffin, M.W. (Eds.): *Behavior Analysis and the Problems of Childhood.* Collingwood, Victoria, Pit Publishing, 1980.

Bettison, S., Davison, D., Taylor, P., and Fox, B.: The long-term effects of a toilet training programme for the retarded: A pilot study. *Australian Journal of Mental Retardation, 4*:28-35, 1976.

Carr, J.: *Helping Your Handicapped Child: A Step-By-Step Guide To Everyday Problems.* Middlesex, England, Penguin Books, 1980.

Foxx, R.M., and Azrin, N.H.: *Toilet Training the Retarded. A Rapid Program for Day and Nighttime Independent Toileting.* Champaign, Illinois, Research Press, 1973.

Giles, D.K., and Wolf, M.M.: Toilet Training in institutionalized, severe retardates: An application of operant behavior modification techniques. *American Journal of Mental Deficiency, 70*:766-780, 1966.

Hamilton, J.: Enviormnental control and retardate behavior. In Rickard, H.C. (Ed.): *Behavioral Intervention in Human Problems.* New York, Pergamon Press, 1971.

Kaines, I.: *A Manual for Toilet Training Using Electronic Alarms.* Adelaide, South Australia, South Australian Institute of Developmental Disabilities, Inc., 1979.

Krumboltz, J.D., and Krumboltz, H.B.: *Changing Children's Behavior.* Englewood Cliffs, Prentice-Hall, 1972.

Larsen, L.A., and Bricker, W.A.: *A Manual for Parents and Teachers of Severely and Moderately Retarded Children* (IMRID Papers V, No. 22). Nashville, IMRID, 1968.

Mahoney, K., Van Wagenen, R.K., and Meyerson, L.: Toilet Training of normal and retarded children. *Journal of Applied Behavior Analysis, 4*:173-181, 1971.

Smith, P.S.: A comparison of different methods of toilet training the mentally handicapped. *Behaviour Research and Therapy, 17*:33-43, 1979.

Smith, P.S., Britton, D.G., Johnson, M., and Thomas, D.A.: Problems involved in toilet training profoundly mentally handicapped adults. *Behaviour Research and Therapy, 13:*301-307, 1975.

Tierney, A.J.: Toilet training. *Nursing Times, 27:*1740-1745, 1973.

Thompson, T., and Grabowski, J. (Eds.): *Behavior Modification of the Mentally Retarded.* New York, Oxford University Press, 1972.

Van Wagenen, R.K., Meyerson, L., Kerr, N.J., and Mahoney, K.: Field trials of new procedure for toilet training. *Journal of Experimental Child Psychology, 8:*147-159, 1969.

Watson, L.S. Jr.: *Child Behavior Modification: A Manual for Teachers, Nurses, and Parents.* New York, Pergamon Press, 1973.

You Also May Be Interested In:

Issam B. Amary—THE RIGHTS OF THE MEN-TALLY RETARDED/DEVELOPMENTALLY DISABLED TO TREATMENT AND EDUCATION. 216 pp., 6 il., $17.50

Caroline Hastings Babington—PARENTING AND THE RETARDED CHILD. 196 pp., 26 il., $16.95

Stephen E. Breuning & Alan D. Poling—DRUGS AND MENTAL RETARDATION. 496 pp., 40 il., 13 tables, about $44.75

Francis Benedict Buda—THE NEUROLOGY OF DEVELOPMENTAL DISABILITIES. 280 pp., 33 il., 16 tables, $27.50

Cynthia D. Crain—MOVEMENT AND RHYTHMIC ACTIVITIES FOR THE MENTALLY RETARDED. 136 pp., 38 il., 4 tables, $14.75

H. D. Bud Fredericks, et al.—THE TEACHING RESEARCH CURRICULUM FOR MODERATELY AND SEVERELY HANDICAPPED: GROSS AND FINE MOTOR. 264 pp. (6⅛ x 9¼), 23 il., 5 tables, $17.75, paper. DEVELOPMENTAL CHART (25 x 19), $3.50

H. D. Bud Fredericks, et al.—THE TEACHING RESEARCH CURRICULUM FOR MODERATELY AND SEVERELY HANDICAPPED: SELF-HELP AND COGNITIVE. 280 pp. (6⅛ x 9¼), 59 il., 5 tables, $17.75, paper. DEVELOPMENTAL CHART (25 x 19), $3.50

Demos Gallender—TEACHING EATING AND TOILETING SKILLS TO THE MULTI-HANDI-CAPPED IN THE SCHOOL SETTING. 384 pp., 12 il., 5 tables, $22.75

Larry Hardy, Garry Martin, Dickie Yu, Clarice Leader & Gordon Quinn—OBJECTIVE BEHAVIORAL ASSESSMENT OF THE SEVERELY AND MODERATELY MENTALLY HANDICAPPED: THE OBA. 136 pp. (8½ x 11), 1 table, $14.75, spiral (paper)

Lous Heshusius—MEANING IN LIFE AS EXPERIENCED BY PERSONS LABELED RETARDED IN A GROUP HOME: A Participant Observation Study. 176 pp., 11 il., 8 tables, cloth-$19.50, paper-$15.75

Jerry Jacobs—MENTAL RETARDATION: A Phenomenological Approach. 244 pp., 1 il., 5 tables, cloth-$24.50, paper-$16.75

Ellen M. Kissinger—A SEQUENTIAL CURRICULUM FOR THE SEVERELY AND PROFOUNDLY MENTALLY RETARDED/MULTI-HANDICAPPED. 276 pp. (11 x 8½), $22.75, spiral (paper)

Victor S. Lombardo—PARAPROFESSIONALS WORKING WITH THE SEVERELY AND PROFOUNDLY RETARDED: Infancy Through Adulthood. 162 pp., 2 il., 1 table, $21.75

Dennis E. Mithaug—PREVOCATIONAL TRAINING FOR RETARDED STUDENTS. 384 pp., 28 il., 27 tables, $29.50

Byron C. Moore, Jane D. Haynes & Clarence R. Laing—INTRODUCTION TO MENTAL RETARDATION SYNDROMES AND TERMINOLOGY. 184 pp., cloth-$14.50, paper-$8.75

David Moxley, Nevalyn Nevil & Barbara Edmonson—SOCIALIZATION GAMES FOR MENTALLY RETARDED ADOLESCENTS AND ADULTS. 130 pp., 18 il., $12.75, spiral (paper)

Olga F. Pader—A GUIDE AND HANDBOOK FOR PARENTS OF MENTALLY RETARDED CHILDREN. 268 pp., 2 il., 1 table, $24.50

Cynthia J. Stacy-Scherrer—SKILLS NECESSARY FOR CONTRIBUTIVE FAMILY AND HOME LIVING: Applicable to the Moderately to Severely Retarded Child and Adult: A Task Analysis Manual for Teachers, Parents, and Houseparents. 390 pp. (8½ x 11), $26.75, spiral (paper)

Sara R. Walsh & Robert Holzberg—UNDERSTANDING AND EDUCATING THE DEAF-BLIND/SEVERELY AND PROFOUNDLY HANDICAPPED: An International Perspective. 328 pp., 29 il., 6 tables, $27.75

Clark Wambold, Roberta Bailey & Deborah Nicholson—INSTRUCTIONAL PROGRAMS AND ACTIVITIES FOR THE SEVERELY HANDICAPPED. 238 pp. (8½ x 11), 48 il., $27.50, spiral (paper)

CHARLES C THOMAS • PUBLISHER
2600 South First Street • Springfield • Illinois • 62717 • USA
(217) 789-8980